STAR COMMAND

THE ART OF

Disney · PIXAR

LIGHTYEAR

FOREWORD BY Andrew Stanton

INTRODUCTION BY Angus MacLane

CHRONICLE BOOKS

SAN FRANCISCO

FRONT COVER TIM EVATT, digital

BACK COVER TIM EVATT, digital

FRONT FLAP DEAN KELLY, digital

BACK FLAP DEAN KELLY, digital

ENDSHEETS GREG PELTZ, digital

PAGE 1 PAUL CONRAD, digital

PAGES 2-3 GREG PELTZ, digital

THIS SPREAD TIM EVATT, digital

FOLLOWING SPREAD TIM EVATT, digital

Library of Congress Cataloging-
in-Publication Data is available.

ISBN 9-1-7972-0084-2
Manufactured in China.

Design by Liam Flanagan.

10 9 8 7 6 5 4 3 2 1

Chronicle Books LLC
680 Second Street
San Francisco, California 94107

CONTENTS

FOREWORD

"Wait—what if he repeats his back story, word-for-word!"

The room broke into laughter, everyone shouting over one another trying to pitch the most iconic space creed possible. This is how I remember the first steps of Buzz Lightyear's world being created—the gag of making the toy Buzz utter, with full conviction, exactly what was written on the back of his toy packaging once he came to life. That was long ago in 1993, and even though the word "meta" would not enter the lexicon for another decade, we all knew we had sparked a conceit bigger than our movie *Toy Story* could hold.

The idea kept growing. What if Buzz Lightyear was an action figure from Andy's favorite TV show? What if this show was a Saturday morning cartoon sci-fi, adventure series? What if we opened *Toy Story* within the Buzz Lightyear show, at the harrowing climax of an episode, and Andy is watching it with his toys?

The idea got very far, but ultimately dramatizing Andy's love for Woody before the cowboy doll's world turned upside-down became a much more important priority. Still, the genie was out of the bottle once Buzz's world was tasted. (You saw us indulge in it briefly at the beginning of *Toy Story 2.*) All of us wanted an excuse to dive headfirst, 100%, into the original world of Buzz Lightyear's character, but no excuse ever came . . .

. . . until Angus. Bless his geek heart.

Nearly twenty years later, director Angus MacLane pitched us his private dream of fully experiencing Buzz Lightyear's world. It was inspired. For Angus, tonally, it would be an amalgamation of all our favorite action-adventures that formed us—*Jonny Quest*, *Star Wars*, *Raiders of the Lost Ark*, *Aliens*—but most of all, it would be legit. Angus drew from a deeper well of details that we had not even considered: rules, complexities, and relationships that gave it an air of authenticity all its own. There was nothing silly or deluded about this Buzz or the future he came from. This Buzz was cool. Still adorkable, yes, but he kicked ass. Andy (aka, us) would have definitely begged his mom for a Buzz Lightyear action figure from this series.

Yep, it was time.

Before you is a book chock full of imagery made by some of the most talented artists today that will finally allow you to visit where we've longed to go for decades. Who knew that "To infinity and beyond" would be so apt a statement for the riches Buzz Lightyear's world had in store. Strap in, Space Rangers, and prepare for lift off . . . .

ANDREW STANTON,
EXECUTIVE PRODUCER
(AND ONE OF BUZZ'S PROUD PARENTS)

GRANT ALEXANDER,
digital

INTRODUCTION

My love of movies began early. I was four years old when I first saw the original *Star Wars* at the Westgate Theater in Beaverton, Oregon. Like many kids of my generation, it was a defining cinematic experience.

I loved the story and the characters, but even more, I was drawn to the art and the design behind it. I studied the *Star Wars* storybook and pop-up book. I poured over any available *Star Wars* imagery, immersing myself in the design of the characters, props, and sets. The officially licensed toy line from Kenner was a design world unto itself, which inspired in me a lifelong love of and appreciation for toys.

The massive success of *Star Wars* inspired a deluge of sci-fi comic books, films, and TV shows, which expanded my concept of science-fiction design. Whenever I would see something captivating, I would file it away in my brain to my mental "oh that's cool" list, hoping that one day I could put a lifetime of design obsession into one movie. When I embarked on the journey of *Lightyear*, I had ideas about the visual language and look I wanted for the film, synthesized from all those years of compiling stunning visuals in my head.

I was fortunate enough to have an incredible team to work with to take those initial ideas, and not just make them a reality, but make them cooler than I ever imagined.

At the very beginning of an animated feature, it's helpful to have a set of visual goals. For *Lightyear*, I had two major areas of design focus that drove the development of the look of the film.

The first design principle we call "chunk." I wanted the world to be tactile and chunky like the live-action science-fiction films that I grew up watching. Before computer generated imagery (CGI) even the lowest-budgeted sci-fi films had wonderfully realized props, sets, and spaceship models that felt functional and real, because they had to be physically built. It's difficult and time-consuming in CGI to make everything feel manufactured and substantial, but the team did an amazing job of designing and building a world that looks and feels tangible.

The second design idea we call the "cinematic" look. I love the high-contrast, moody, and visually striking frames of artists like Douglas Slocombe, Adrian Biddle, Henri Decaë, and Gordon Willis. Inspired by their masterworks, I wanted to use shadow and contrast to direct the eye and create a cinematic atmosphere.

When making CGI animated films, everything on screen needs to be designed and built from scratch. Thus there is a tendency to want to highlight and feature every element, regardless of its importance in telling the story, because it took so long to create. However for *Lightyear*, I wanted to emulate the simplicity and boldness of some of my favorite cinematic moments. When I think back on the most indelible images from my favorite films, they aren't that complex. Think of Luke

Skywalker looking at the twin suns of Tatooine in *Star Wars*, Indiana Jones running from the boulder in *Raiders of the Lost Ark*, Ripley in the power loader emerging from the docking bay to battle with the alien queen in *Aliens*. Simple, unforgettable visual scenes with a clear graphic focus. That was my goal.

The crew of *Lightyear* built beautiful characters, props, and sets, and then often the lighting and effects teams obscured much of that terrific work, all with the final film frame in mind. The results are breathtaking.

This "Art of" book represents only a small fraction of the work produced by this extremely talented team of artists over a six-year period. We took these two principles, the "chunk" and the "cinematic" looks, and aimed to make a movie world that is not necessarily realistic, but is believable.

I couldn't be prouder of the work, and I will be forever grateful to the artists who brought their immense talent and generosity to *Lightyear*. I hope that the following pages of "cinematic chunk" inspire you the way they inspired me.

ANGUS MacLANE,
DIRECTOR

RESEARCH

Starting on *Lightyear*, the team headed to Houston's NASA Johnson Space Center on November 12–15, 2019. We were greeted by Tom Marshburn, his family, Kjell N. Lindgren, Nicole Aunapu Mann, and Shaneequa Vereen. They gave us a crash course on space technology and some of the training to become an astronaut. I felt honored to be where the Apollo missions took place and thankful the NASA team took the time to educate us on space flight. The information they provided us with helped inform our choices when creating *Lightyear* so that hopefully the film will feel both grounded and believable while also being fantastical. We could always call up our new resources if we had any questions. This type of research is essential to Pixar and a lot of fun for our crew.

TIM EVATT, Production Designer

THIS SPREAD TIM EVATT, DEAN KELLY, and TOM MARSHBURN, photography

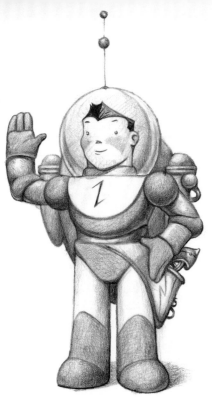

WILLIAM JOYCE, pencil

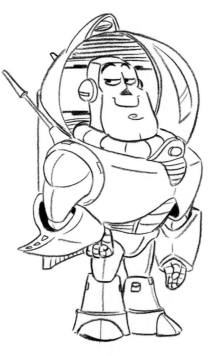

JEFF PIDGEON, pencil

JEFF PIDGEON, pencil

BUD LUCKEY, pencil

BUD LUCKEY, ink and marker

BUD LUCKEY, ink and marker

NILO RODIS, pencil, marker, and gouache

NILO RODIS, pencil, marker, and gouache

BOB PAULEY, colored pencil and marker

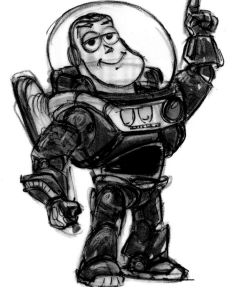

BOB PAULEY, marker and photocopy

Designing Buzz was fun, in fact it was a dream job. Toy truth: For the toy to be believable, Buzz's design had to be faithful to the functionality, construction, material, and scale of an action figure from 1995. For the story, Buzz needed to be a cool toy to contrast, outshine, and challenge Woody and his place on the bed. Referencing US astronaut spacesuits, the design is a cleaner, hard shell construction with an integrated jet pack, communicator, and LED laser. Bright green and purple color accents, badging, and graphics indicate he is not just a toy astronaut but a Space Ranger.

BOB PAULEY, original Buzz Lightyear Designer

RIGHT **BOB PAULEY, pen and photocopy**

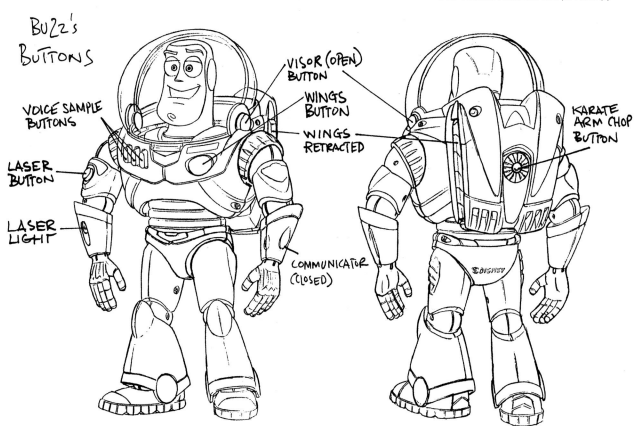

BUZZ'S BUTTONS

VOICE SAMPLE BUTTONS

LASER BUTTON

LASER LIGHT

VISOR (OPEN) BUTTON

WINGS BUTTON

WINGS RETRACTED

COMMUNICATOR (CLOSED)

KARATE ARM CHOP BUTTON

DEAN HEEZAN, digital

MATT NOLTE, colored pencil

DEAN HEEZAN,
digital

18

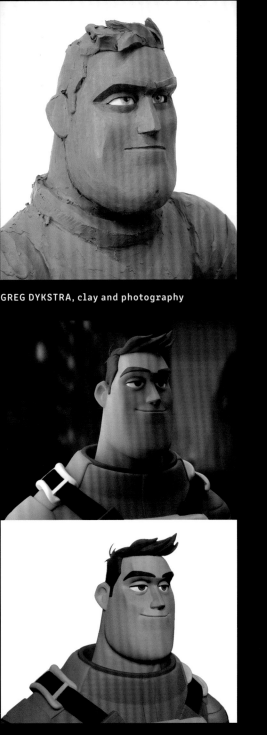

GREG DYKSTRA, clay and photography

KALEB RICE, digital sculpt

GREG DYKSTRA, clay and photography

The challenge in reimagining something so iconic is to broaden or in some cases establish a new vocabulary while holding onto those elements that most resonate with what we know about *Toy Story* Buzz. Because Buzz was a toy there was a physicality to the original design, but we had to take that believability further in order to bring Buzz and his world forward into a more concrete realistic setting. Angus really pushed the team to think about the functionality and mechanics. We wanted a solid, constructed, mechanical reality.

GRANT ALEXANDER, Character Designer

THIS SPREAD GRANT ALEXANDER, digital

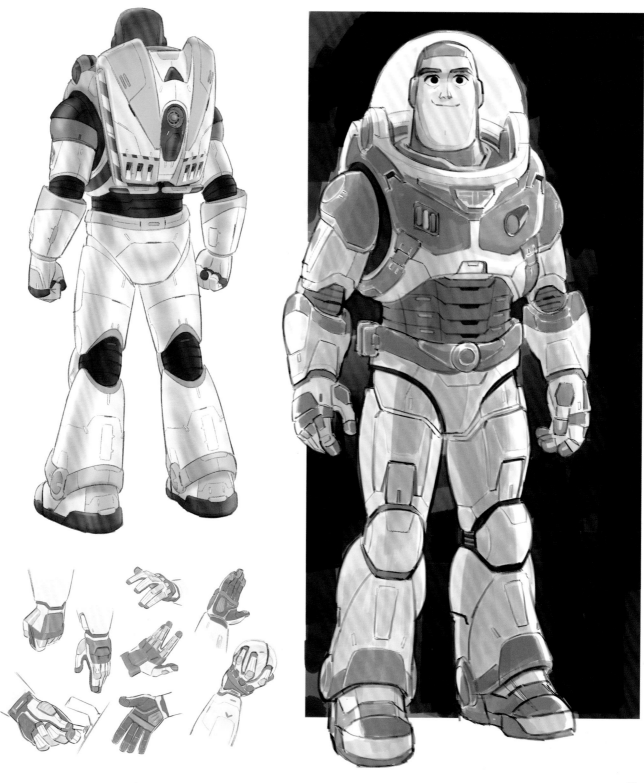

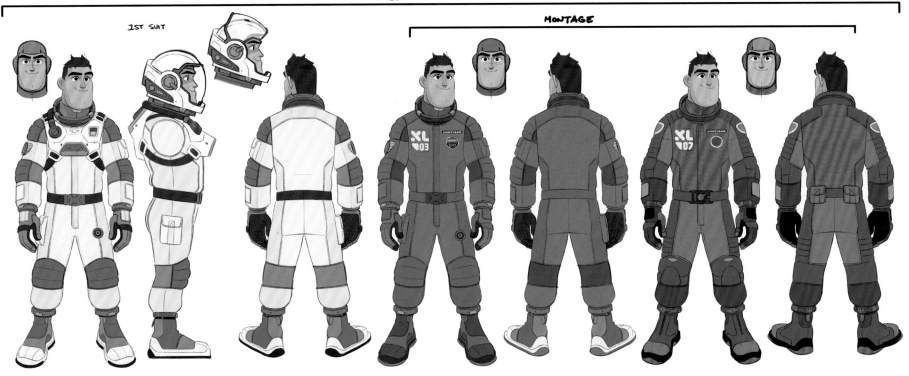

1ST SUIT

MONTAGE

2ND ACT

3RD ACT

JAMMIES

One of the goals with the evolution of the flight suits was to create a look that tied into the world of Buzz stylistically but was also reminiscent of the Space Race era and used materials that were familiar enough that the suits and their fabrics made logical sense. We also wanted to distinguish each era with a unique color palette, with the hope that any suit could be recognizable and easily tied to a particular flight.

BILL ZAHN, Shading Art Director

THIS PAGE DEAN HEEZEN, digital

CALUM ALEXANDER WATT, digital

FLIGHT SUIT

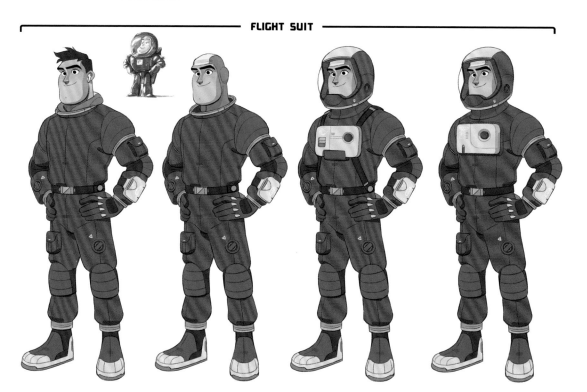

DEAN HEEZEN, digital

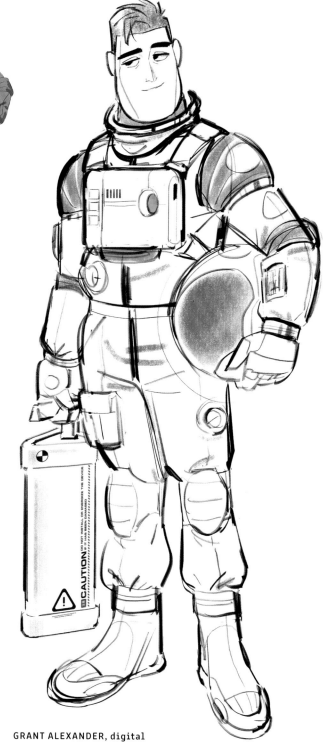

GRANT ALEXANDER, digital

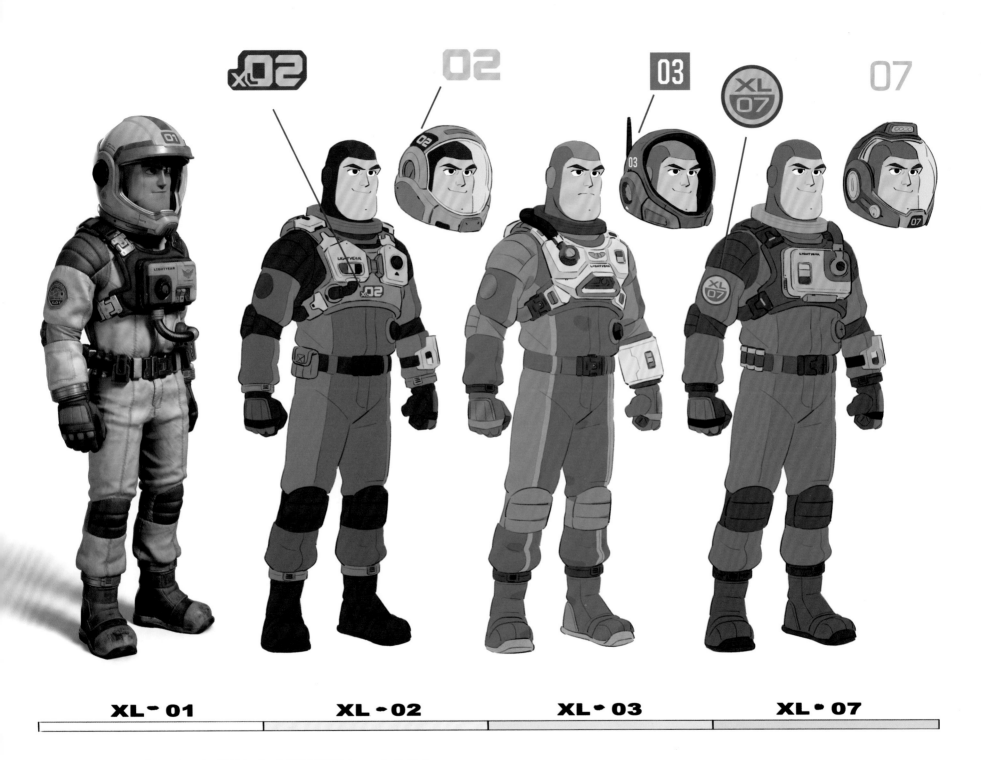

XL - 01   XL - 02   XL • 03   XL • 07

XL-01 ETHAN DEAN and GEORGE NGUYEN (shading); BEN PORTER (groom): digital

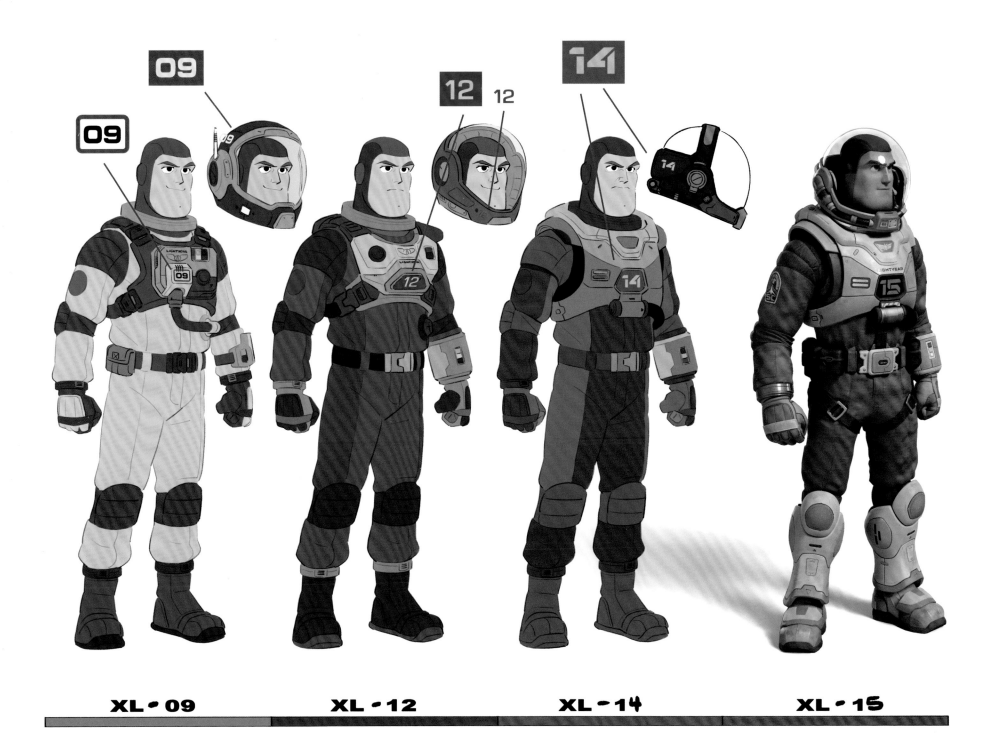

XL•09   **XL•12**   **XL•14**   **XL•15**

XL-02—XL-14 DEAN HEEZEN (design); BILL ZAHN (color): digital

XL-15 CHRIS HARVEY (shading); BEN PORTER (groom): digital

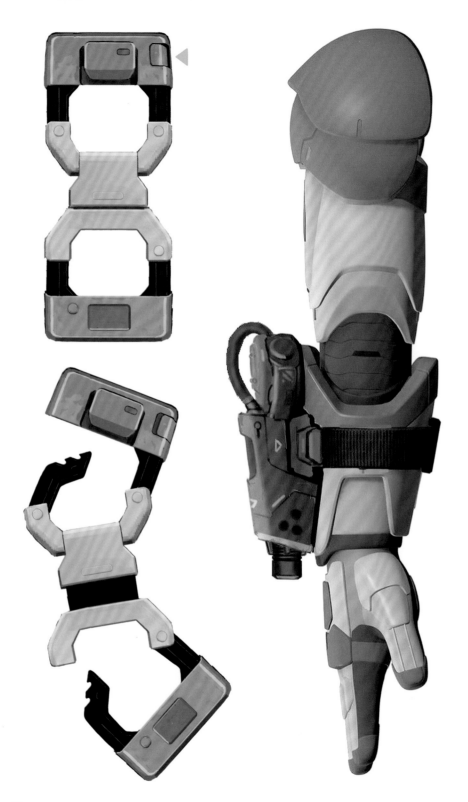

FAR LEFT
MATT NOLTE, digital

LEFT AND ABOVE
GRANT ALEXANDER, digital

26

GRANT ALEXANDER (design); DAVE STRICK and JACOB SPEIRS (model);
PAUL CONRAD (graphics); STACEY TRUMAN (shading): digital

CALUM ALEXANDER WATT, digital

CASUAL   **CASUAL JUMPER**   **FLIGHT JUMPER**

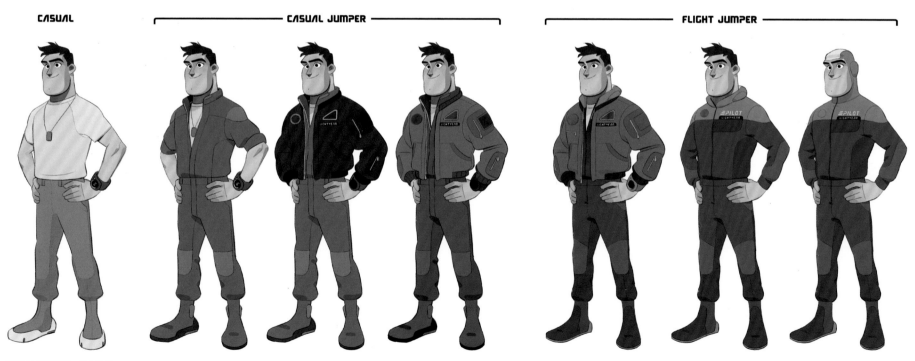

DEAN HEEZEN, digital

DEAN HEEZEN, digital

KALEB RICE, digital

DEAN HEEZEN, digital

DEAN HEEZEN, digital

KALEB RICE, digital

MATT NOLTE,
pencil and watercolor

DEAN KELLY, digital

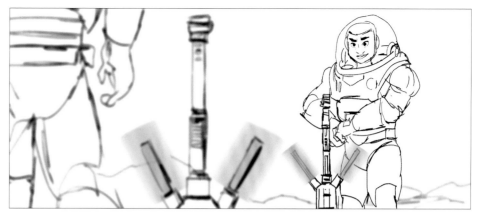

DEAN KELLY, digital

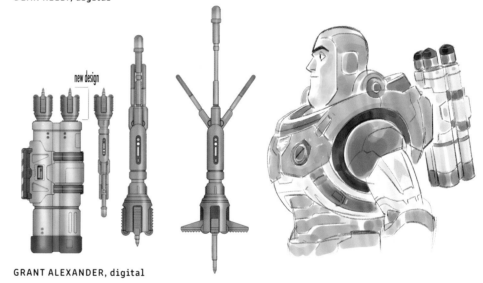

new design

GRANT ALEXANDER, digital

SPACE RANGER ACADEMY

MARGARET SPENCER, digital

MATT NOLTE,
digital

ABOVE MARGARET SPENCER, digital

We don't get to see much of Alisha's life while Buzz embarks on his missions, so I came up with some ideas about her grand-daughter Izzy's upbringing and how her grandmother influenced her. We explored this idea that Izzy was a "Planet Ranger," and that, while Buzz always had an aversion to the dangerous planet, Alisha eventually grew to appreciate it and helped her granddaughter learn to admire it as well.

MARGARET SPENCER, Story Artist

LEFT MATT NOLTE, digital

I was thrilled to shade Alisha as she is not only a strong female lead character but also Buzz's best friend and mentor. Alisha's unique design needed to show the passing of time through her age progression. I developed her skin tone by shifting the hue and value and adding minimal blemishes in order to age her gracefully. And when shading her in 3D, I adjusted her color and displacement paint for each age variant of her model. Thanks to strong collaboration between the art and shading teams, I had the opportunity to both design Alisha's paint in 2D and then seamlessly carry it into her 3D paint and shading.

MARIA LEE, Shading Artist

RIGHT MARIA LEE, digital

BELOW SOFYA OGUNSEITAN, digital

Young (35)　　**Older (45)**　　**Older (65)**　　**Oldest (75)**

DEAN HEEZEN, digital

ANGUS MacLANE and MARGARET SPENCER, digital

MATT NOLTE, digital

RANDY BERRETT, digital

ABOVE RANDY BERRETT, digital

RIGHT MARGARET SPENCER, digital

35

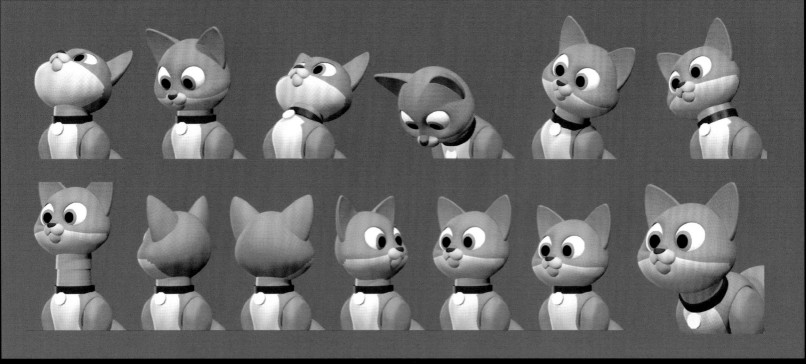

KALEB RICE, digital

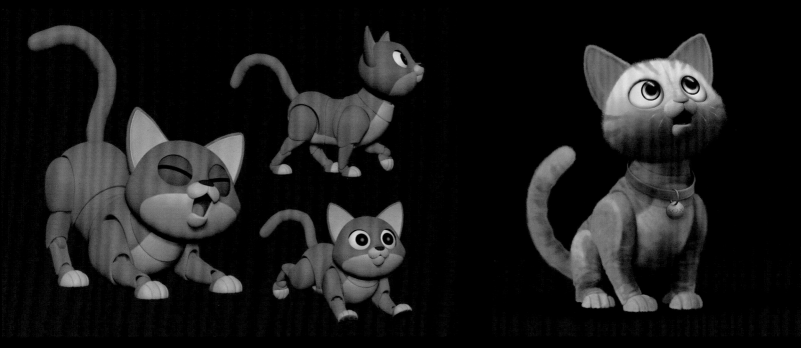

KALEB RICE, digital

KALEB RICE (sculpt); BILL ZAHN (shading): digital

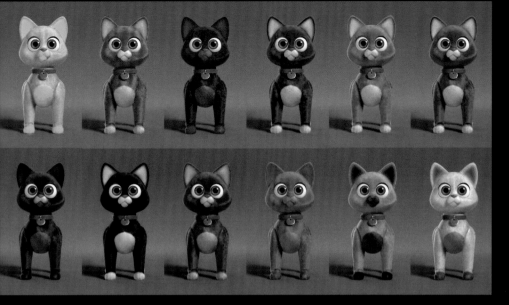

HANG IN THERE

DEAN HEEZEN, digital

GRANT ALEXANDER, digital

GRANT ALEXANDER, digital

In the film Izzy needed to become Buzz Lightyear's best friend. She needed to be full of life and humor, and strong where Buzz was weak. She also needed to be very empathetic and someone that could be a teacher to Buzz. All these things had to come across in her design. Thank goodness this is a collaborative art form. All of the character designers on this film helped find "our Izzy." She is the result of a lot of thought and care by a lot of friends in the studio—from Art all the way through the rest of the production departments. Izzy's character and design is a reflection of many people's efforts and it suits her well.

MATT NOLTE, Character Art Designer

THIS PAGE MATT NOLTE, pencil and digital color

THIS PAGE DEAN HEEZEN, digital

MARIA LEE, digital

CALUM ALEXANDER
WATT, digital

GRANT ALEXANDER, digital

CORY LOFTIS, digital

DEAN HEEZEN, digital

BOBBY ALCID RUBIO, digital

CHARLES CHOO JR., digital

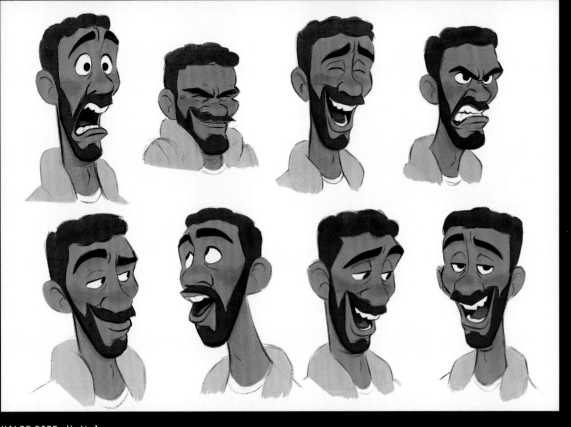

KALEB RICE, digital

MARIA LEE, digital

KALEB RICE, digital sculpt

CORY LOFTIS, digital

CALUM ALEXANDER WATT, digital

CORY LOFTIS, digital

MATT NOLTE, pencil

MATT NOLTE, digital

MATT NOLTE, pencil

MARIA LEE, digital

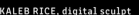

KALEB RICE, digital sculpt

WEAPONS

THIS SPREAD
GRANT ALEXANDER, digital

BOBBY ALCID RUBIO, digital

MATT NOLTE, pencil and digital color

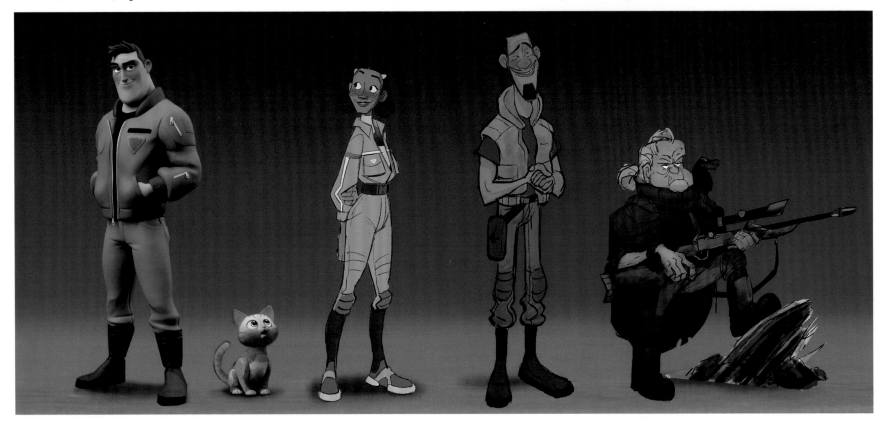

MATT NOLTE, digital

KALEB RICE, digital

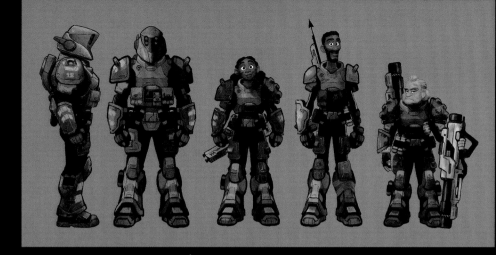

MATT NOLTE, digital

BILL ZAHN, digital shading

Michael Fong had this shorthand way of drawing robots. Drawing the Zyclops character in storyboard form, Michael created these Frankenstein elongated bodies that Angus thought would be great for the final character. Dean Heezen, informed by these drawings, would further flesh out the final character design, which would later be 3D modeled by Michael Neavez.

TIM EVATT, Production Designer

DEAN HEEZEN, digital

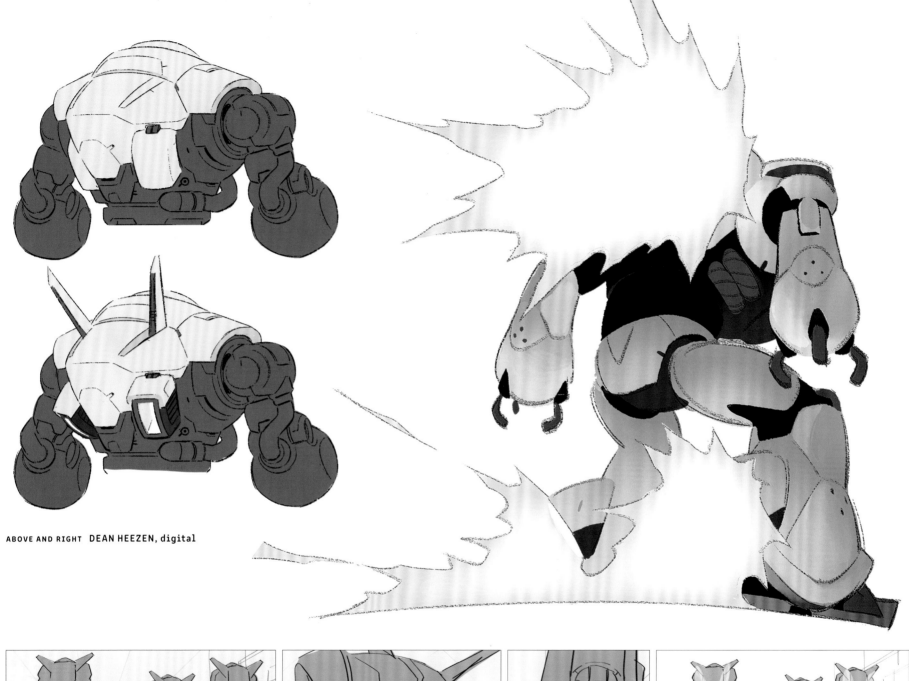

ABOVE AND RIGHT DEAN HEEZEN, digital

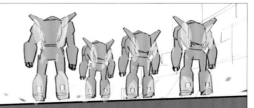

MICHAEL FONG, digital

51

GRANT ALEXANDER, digital

MARGARET SPENCER, digital

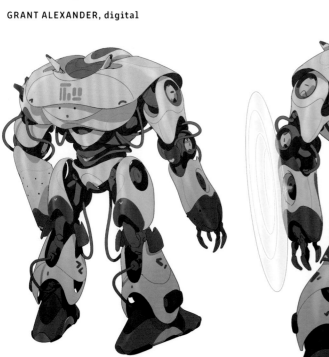

CALUM ALEXANDER WATT, digital

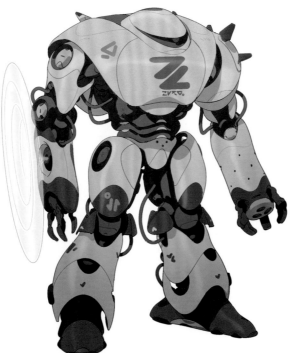

GRANT ALEXANDER, digital

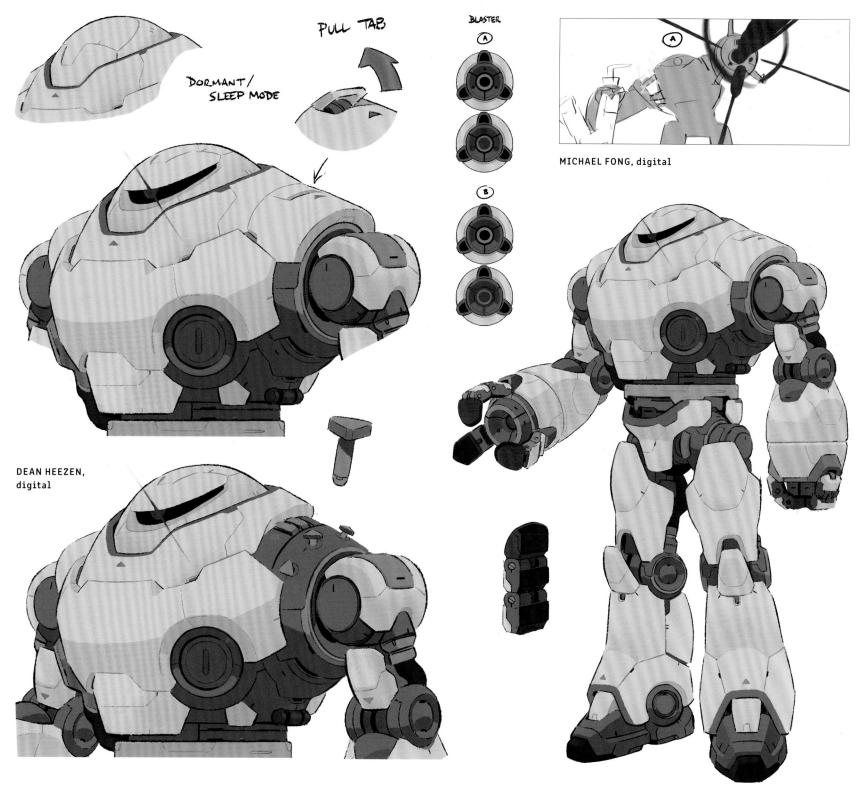

PULL TAB

DORMANT /
SLEEP MODE

BLASTER

A

B

MICHAEL FONG, digital

DEAN HEEZEN,
digital

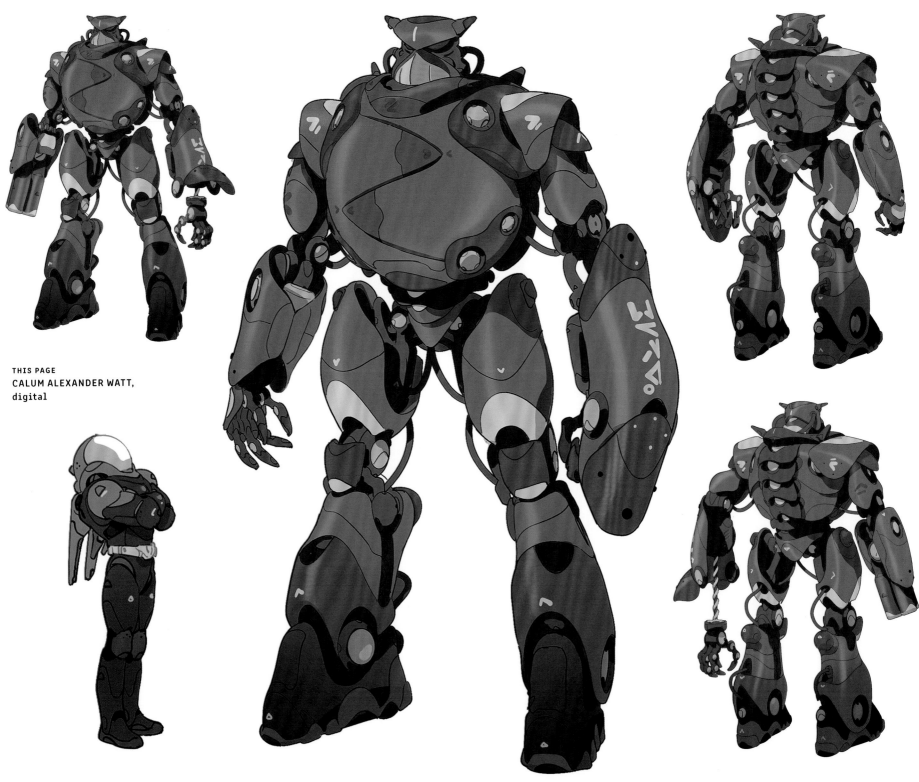

THIS PAGE
CALUM ALEXANDER WATT,
digital

DEAN KELLY, digital

GRANT ALEXANDER, digital

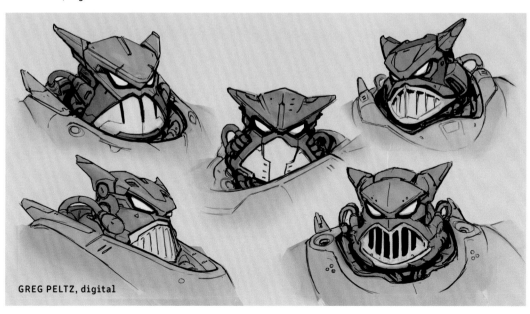

GREG PELTZ, digital

GREG PELTZ, digital

55

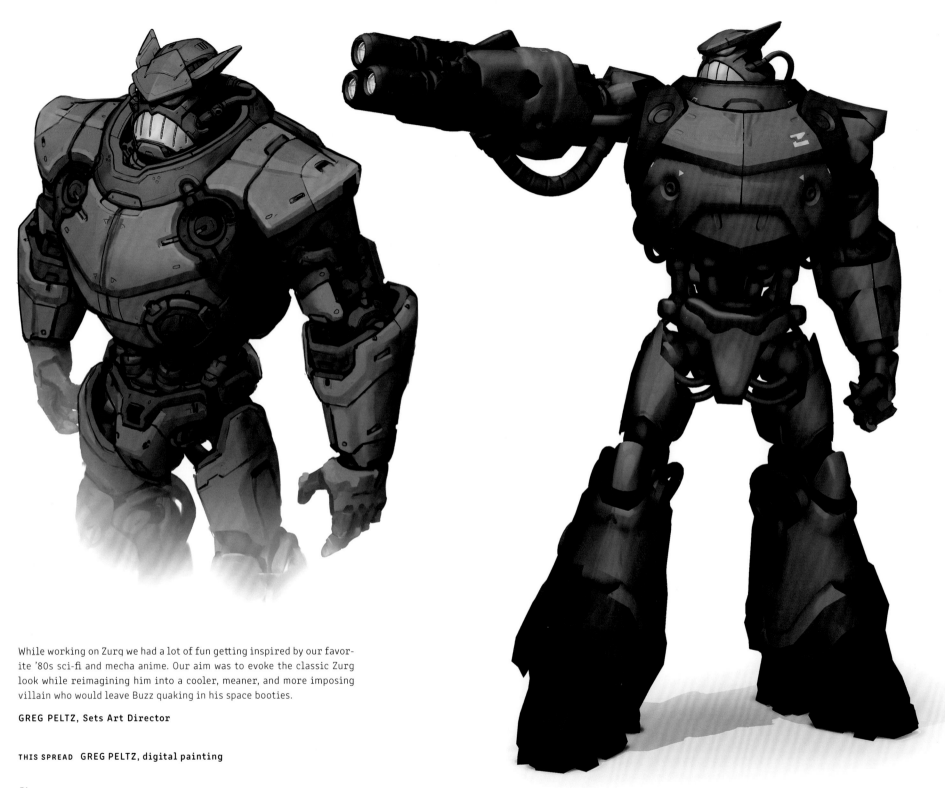

While working on Zurg we had a lot of fun getting inspired by our favorite '80s sci-fi and mecha anime. Our aim was to evoke the classic Zurg look while reimagining him into a cooler, meaner, and more imposing villain who would leave Buzz quaking in his space booties.

GREG PELTZ, Sets Art Director

THIS SPREAD GREG PELTZ, digital painting

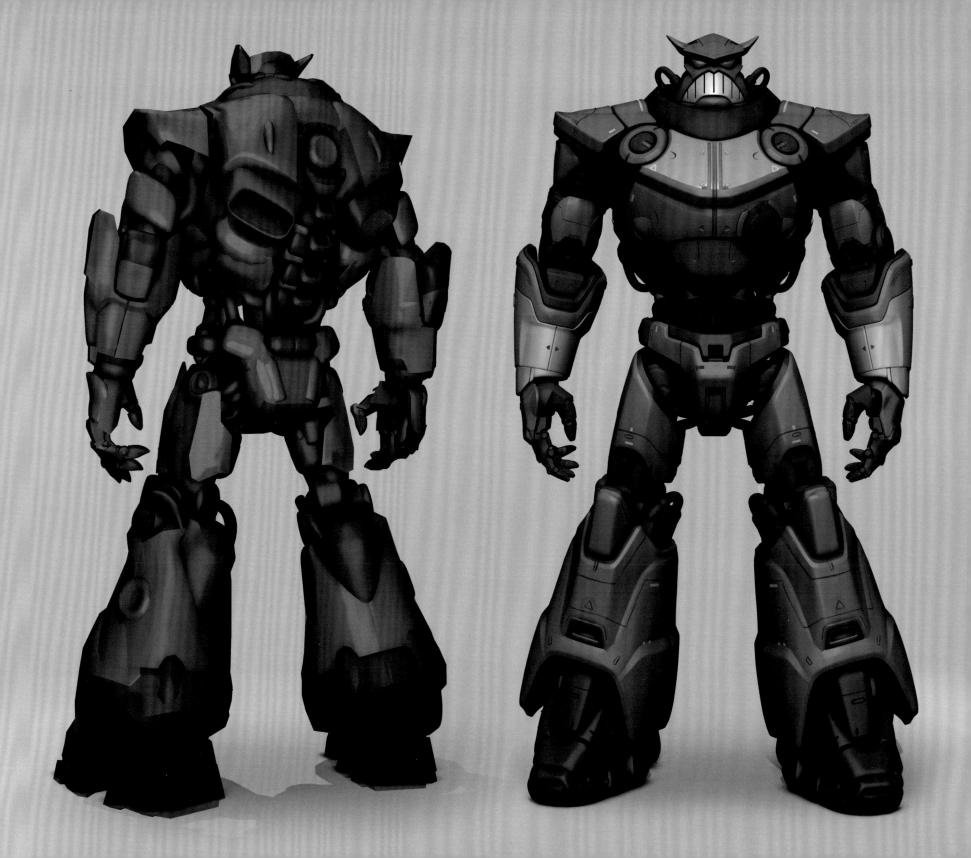

ABOVE AND LEFT
DEAN HEEZEN, digital

BELOW AND ARM
CALUM ALEXANDER WATT, digital

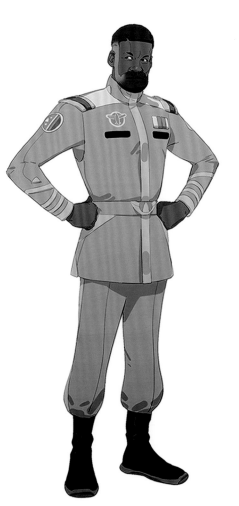

58

DEAN HEEZEN, digital

BOBBY ALCID RUBIO, digital

CHRIS HARVEY (shading); SOFYA OGUNSEITAN (groom): digital

GRANT ALEXANDER, digital

KALEB RICE, digital sculpt

GRANT ALEXANDER, digital

MARIA LEE, digital

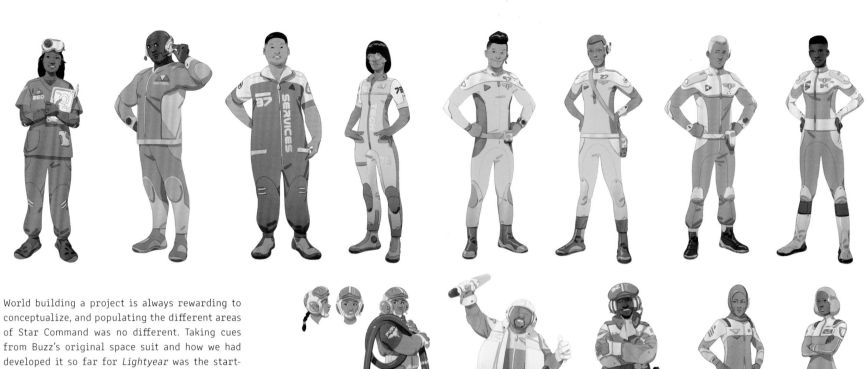

World building a project is always rewarding to conceptualize, and populating the different areas of Star Command was no different. Taking cues from Buzz's original space suit and how we had developed it so far for *Lightyear* was the starting point for me: little signature lines and design elements that could be reflected across Mission Control, Ground Crew, Medical, and Salvage Crew helps to create a convincing ready-built and lived-in world for the viewer.

CALUM ALEXANDER WATT, Development Artist

THIS PAGE CALUM ALEXANDER WATT, digital

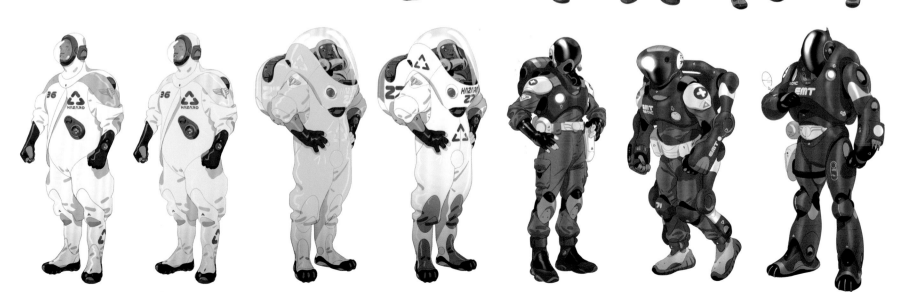

GRANT ALEXANDER, MATT NOLTE, and DEAN HEEZEN, pencil and digital

Matt, Dean, and I spent lunches sketching and collecting unique, individual caricatures to help populate our world. As designers, we're always striving to present fresh, surprising, or novel imagery. In the beginning, we were trying to figure out what made our film different from *Toy Story* and to understand what level of stylization would be appropriate for the film.

GRANT ALEXANDER, Character Designer

MATT NOLTE and GRANT ALEXANDER, digital

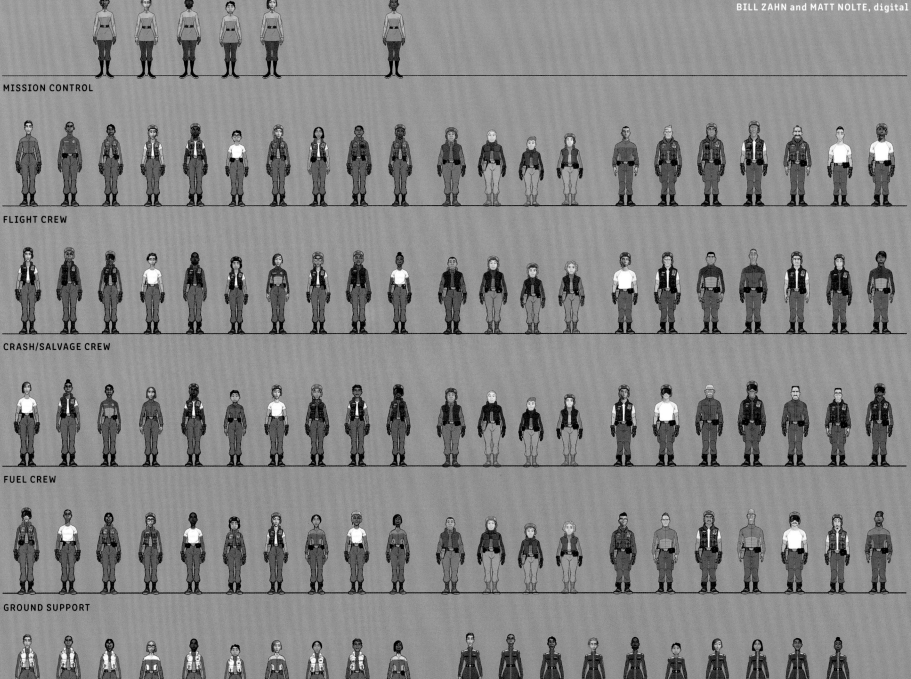

MISSION CONTROL

FLIGHT CREW

CRASH/SALVAGE CREW

FUEL CREW

GROUND SUPPORT

MEDICAL

COMMAND

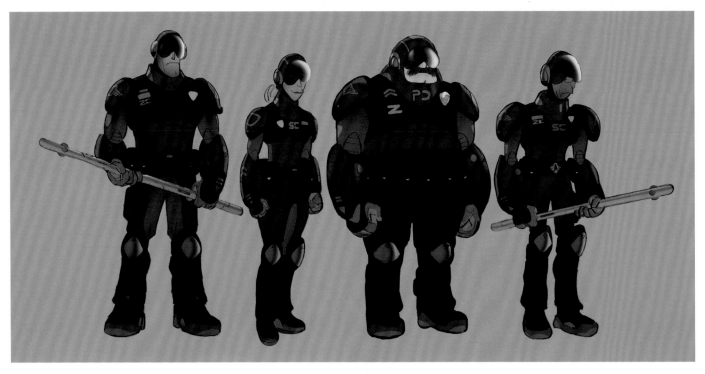

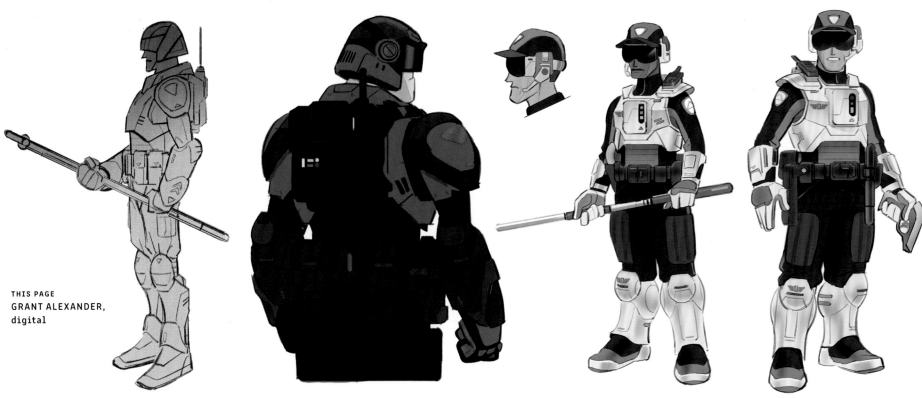

THIS PAGE
GRANT ALEXANDER,
digital

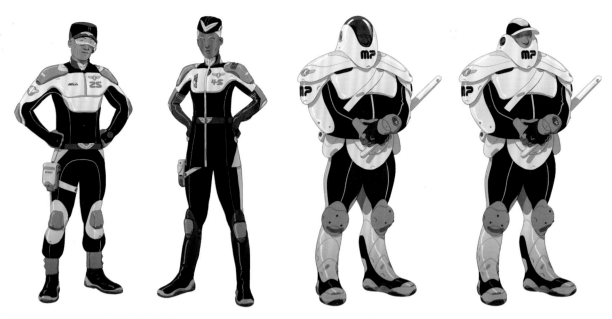

CALUM ALEXANDER WATT, digital

CALUM ALEXANDER WATT, digital

ABOVE   PAUL CONRAD, digital

RIGHT   BRENDA ZHANG (sculpt); ETHAN DEAN
(shading); PAUL CONRAD (graphics): digital

GARRETT TAYLOR, digital

ENVIRONMENTS

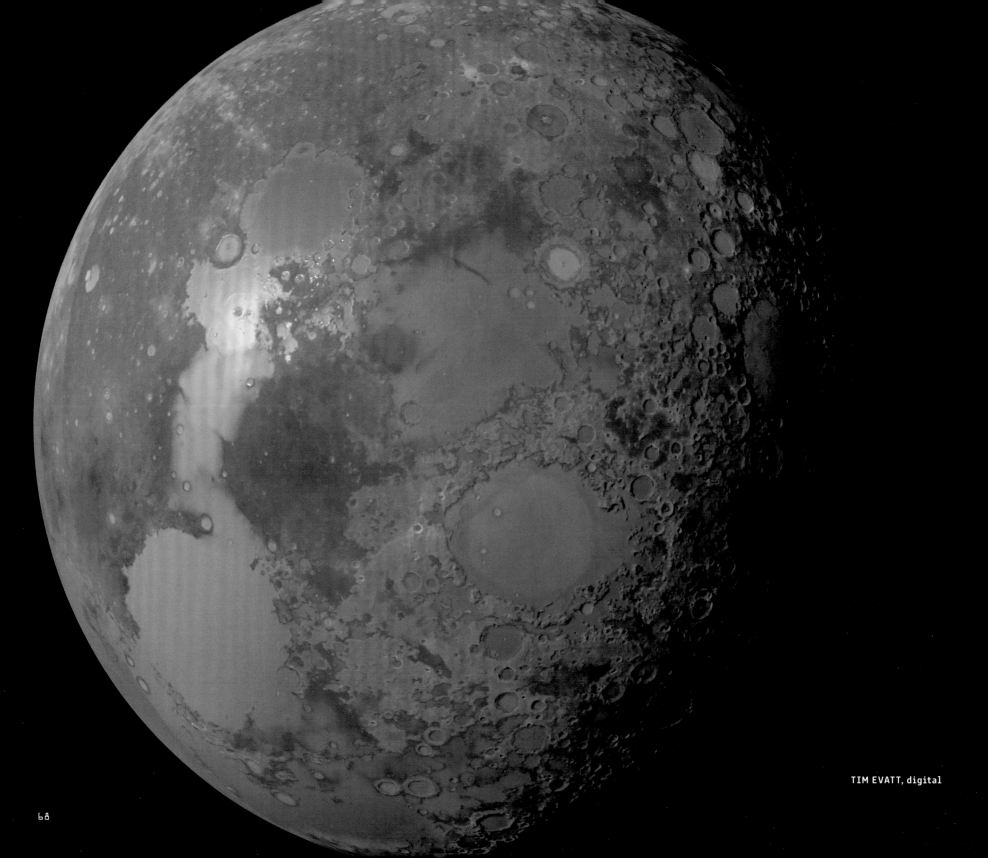

TIM EVATT, digital

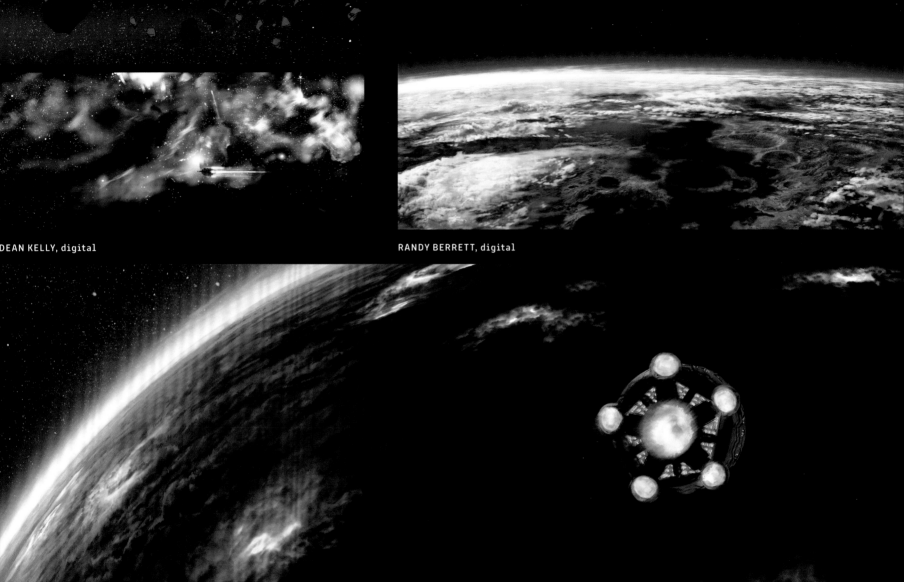

DEAN KELLY, digital

RANDY BERRETT, digital

RANDY BERRETT, digital

GARRETT TAYLOR, digital

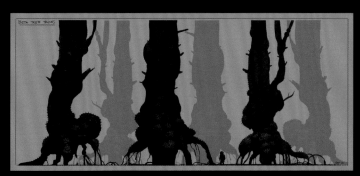

GARRETT TAYLOR, digital

JACY JOHNSON, digital

MATT NOLTE, digital

ROOKIE MISTAKE, PART 1
DEAN KELLY, digital

One of the exciting challenges when you're developing a story is to find the most impactful and captivating way to open the film. It should immediately hook the audience and provide insight as to what they can expect from the rest of the film. We wanted the audience to know this is not Buzz Lightyear the toy. This is Buzz Lightyear the man, and this is his story. We thought the best way to show that would be through an action sequence. We experimented with several dif-ferent openings, but none of them were setting up Buzz and his story in the right way. Once we understood who Alisha's character was, we thought it would be so cool to see Buzz and Alisha as Space Rangers on an exciting mission together. In true sci-fi manner, we used the planet and its inhabitants as the main source of antagonism. It was really exciting to board this opening sequence to set Buzz up in a way audiences have never seen before. **DEAN KELLY, Story Supervisor**

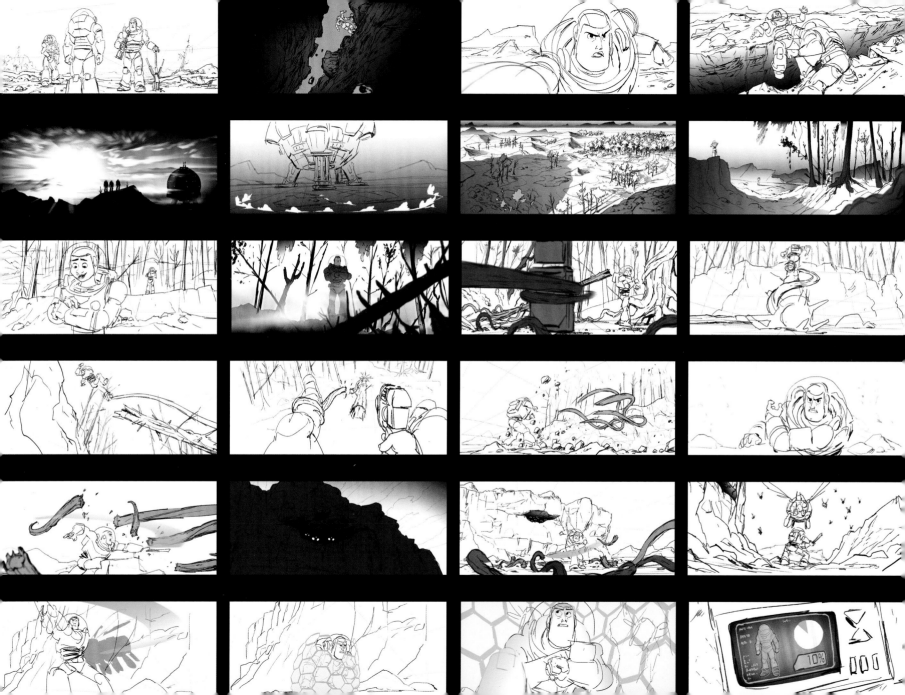

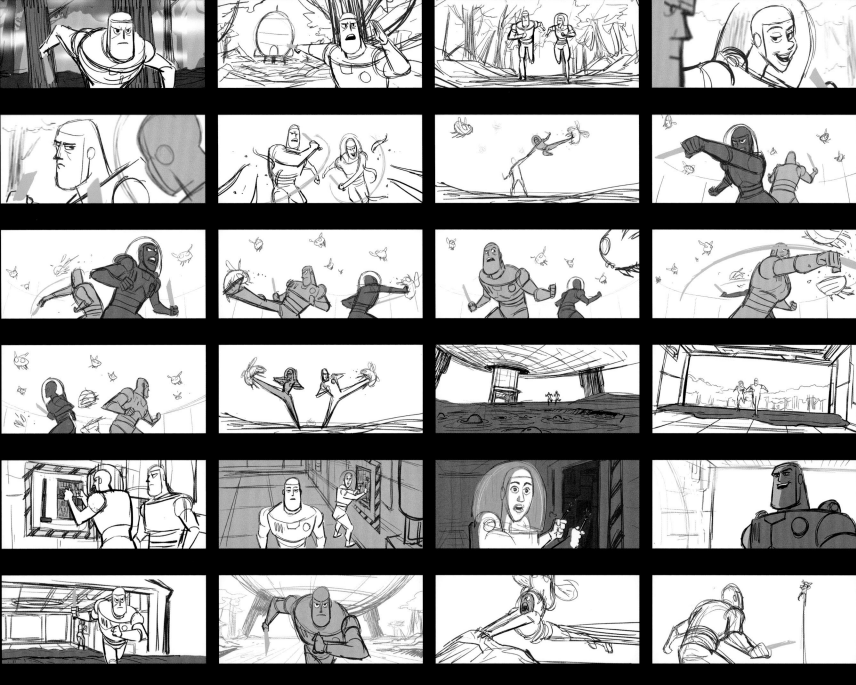

ROOKIE MISTAKE, PART 2
BOBBY ALCID RUBIO, digital

For the second part of the sequence "Rookie Mistake," I was inspired by sci-fi action movies and '80s animated shows that I loved as a kid! It was my opportunity to storyboard the Space Rangers in their prime, and I tried to infuse as much thrill, comedy, and drama into the scene as possible. I kept thinking that this was the movie that Andy from *Toy Story* saw, so it had to be AWESOME, EXCITING, and FULL-THROTTLE FUN!
BOBBY ALCID RUBIO, Story Artist

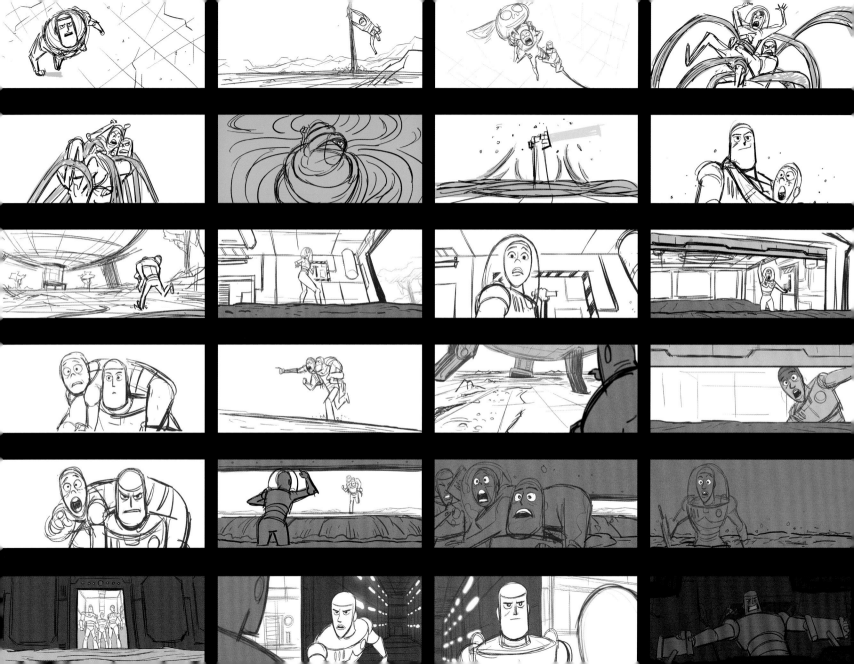

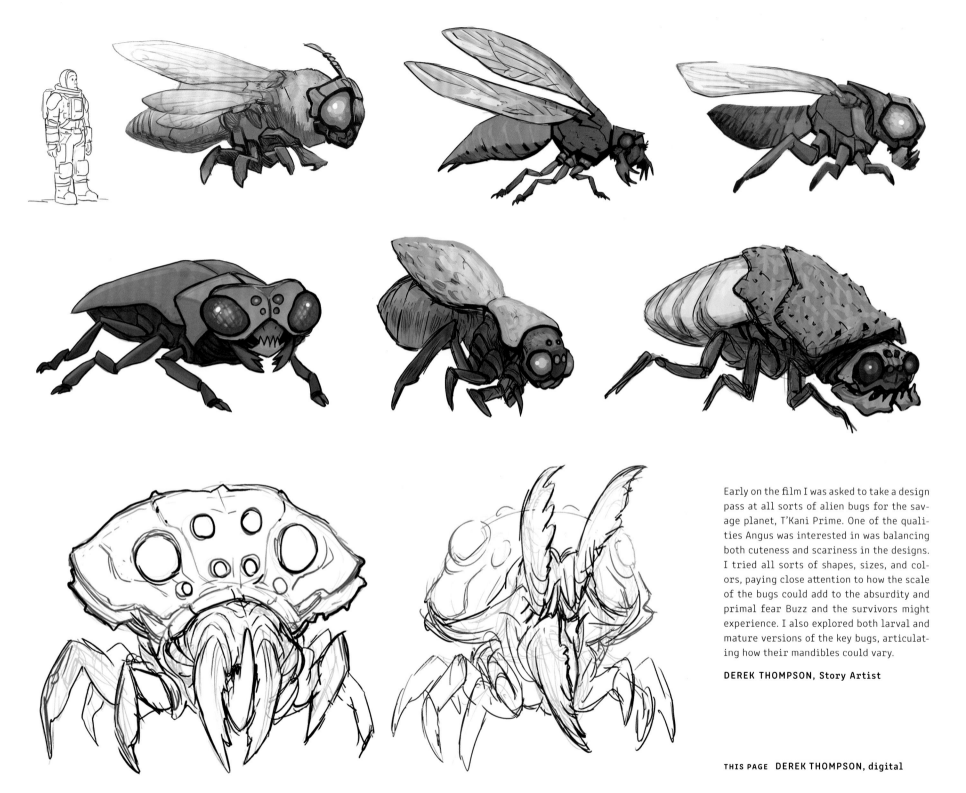

Early on the film I was asked to take a design pass at all sorts of alien bugs for the savage planet, T'Kani Prime. One of the qualities Angus was interested in was balancing both cuteness and scariness in the designs. I tried all sorts of shapes, sizes, and colors, paying close attention to how the scale of the bugs could add to the absurdity and primal fear Buzz and the survivors might experience. I also explored both larval and mature versions of the key bugs, articulating how their mandibles could vary.

DEREK THOMPSON, Story Artist

THIS PAGE DEREK THOMPSON, digital

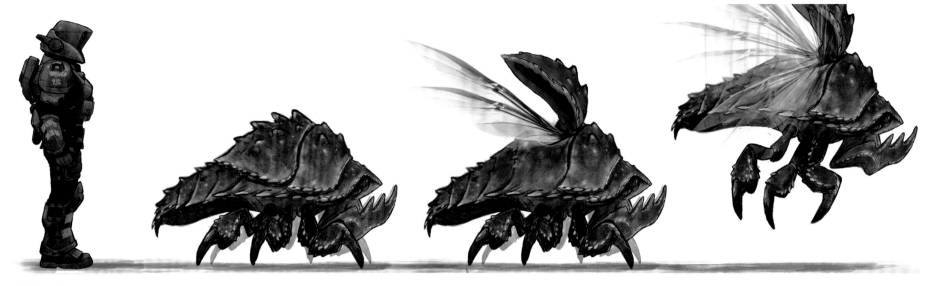

MATT NOLTE, digital

Space Bugs? There are millions of kids out there who would love getting this assignment. There are also millions of ways this could have gone. For *Lightyear*, it was a mixture of crustacean, tick, beetle, wasp, and a bit of ankylosaurus.

MATT NOLTE,
Character Design
Art Director

MATT NOLTE, clay; NICK MIKESELL, photography

TED MATHOT, digital

GREG PELTZ, digital

GARRETT TAYLOR, digital

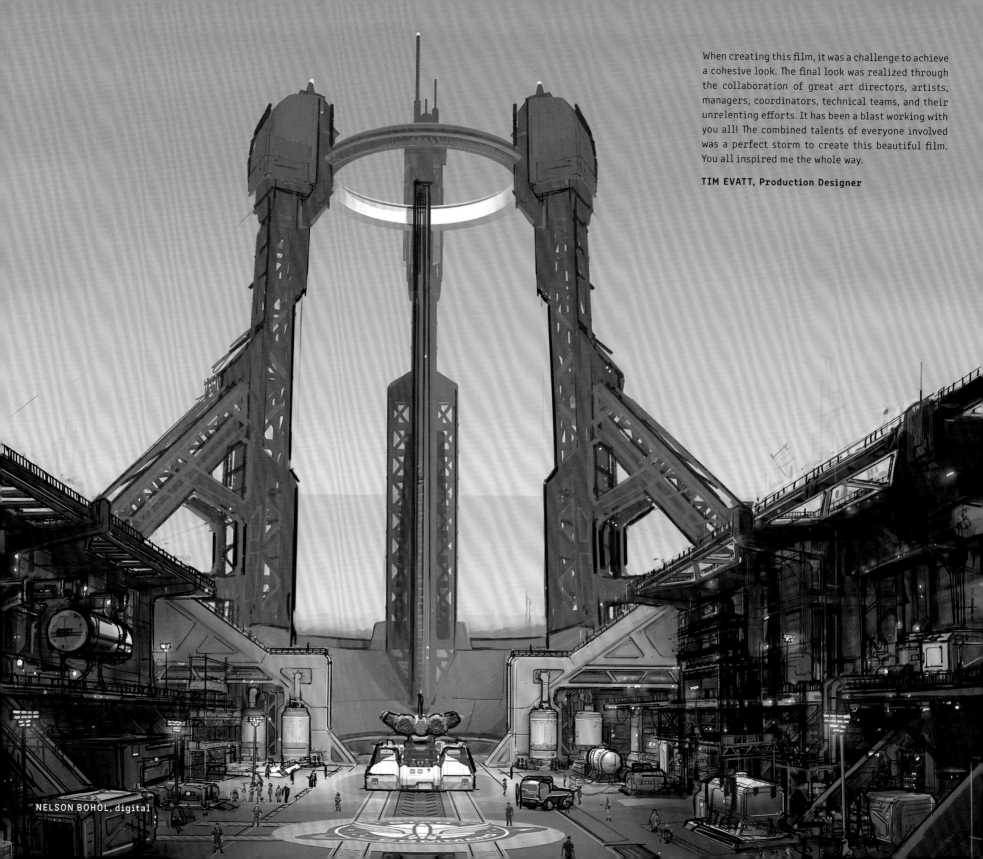

When creating this film, it was a challenge to achieve a cohesive look. The final look was realized through the collaboration of great art directors, artists, managers, coordinators, technical teams, and their unrelenting efforts. It has been a blast working with you all! The combined talents of everyone involved was a perfect storm to create this beautiful film. You all inspired me the whole way.

TIM EVATT, Production Designer

NELSON BOHOL, digital

TIM EVATT, digital

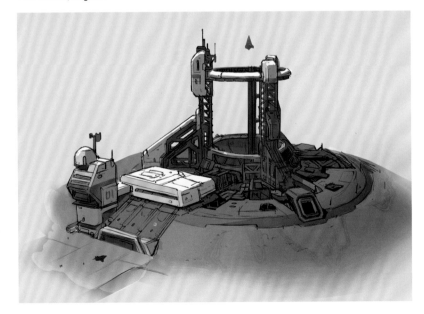

GREG PELTZ, digital

GARRETT TAYLOR, digital

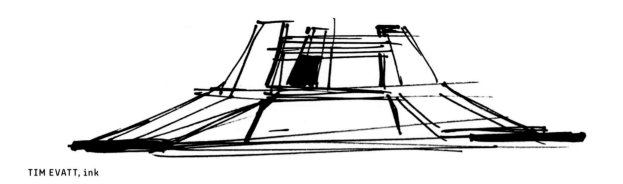

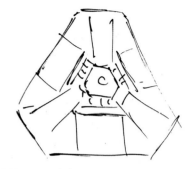

TIM EVATT, ink

GREG PELTZ, ink

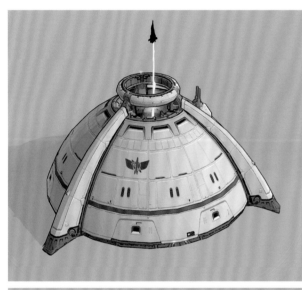

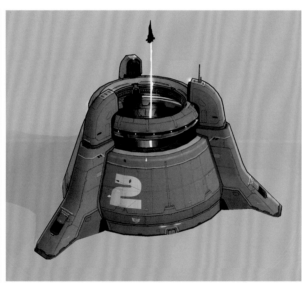

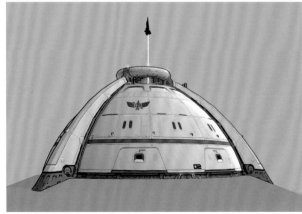

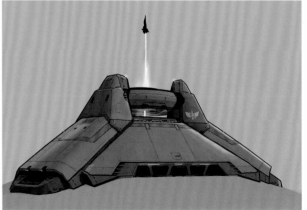

GREG PELTZ, digital

GARRETT TAYLOR, digital

GARRETT TAYLOR, digital

TIM EVATT, digital

GREG PELTZ, digital

TIM EVATT and BILL ZAHN, digital

TIM EVATT, digital

GARRETT TAYLOR, digital

DEAN KELLY, digital

GREG PELTZ, digital

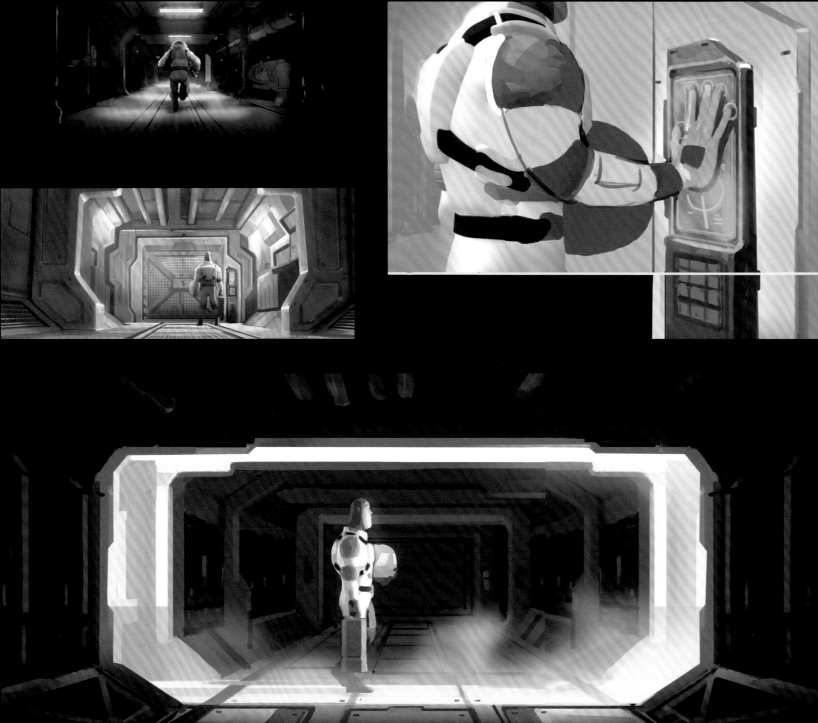

NELSON BOHOL, digital

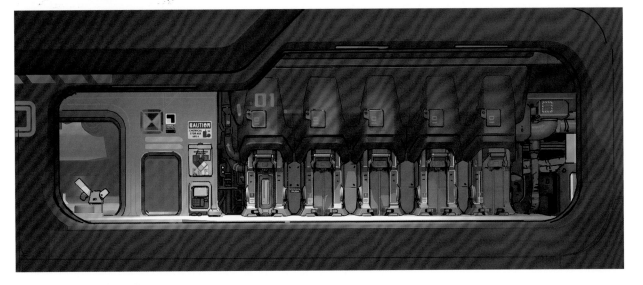

GARRETT TAYLOR, digital

DEAN KELLY, digital

MICHAEL FONG, digital

GREG PELTZ, digital

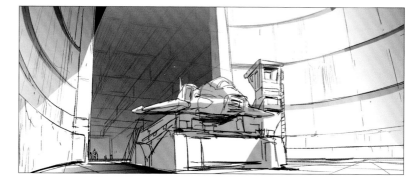

DEAN KELLY, digital

GREG PELTZ, digital

GARRETT TAYLOR, digital

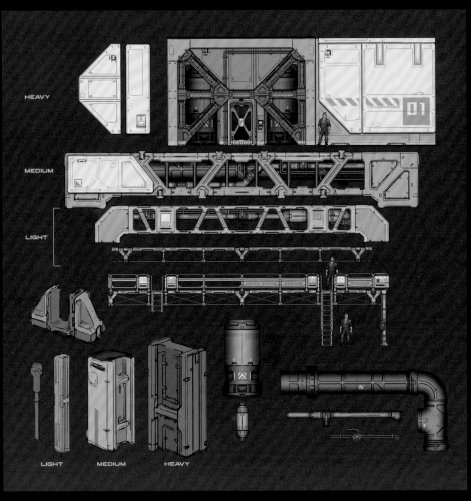

HEAVY

MEDIUM

LIGHT

LIGHT   MEDIUM   HEAVY

GREG PELTZ, digital

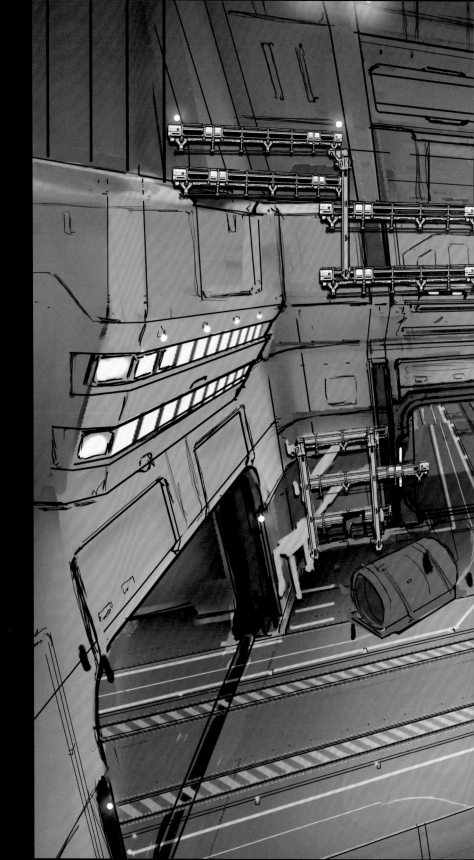

GREG PELTZ, digital

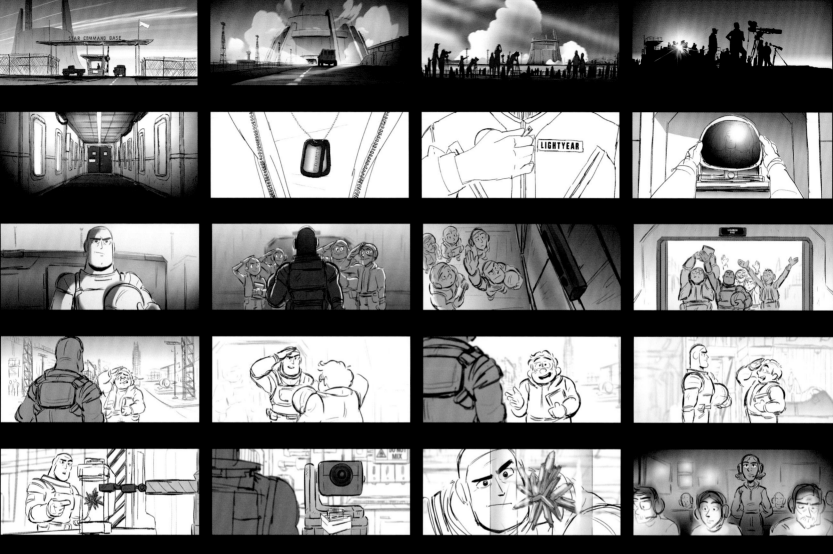

PREFLIGHT

**DEAN KELLY (01–08)
and NICOLLE CASTRO
(09–48), digital**

Preflight is a sequence that has managed to stay in the story in some shape or form since the very beginning. As the story evolves, we start to see there are different elements which need to be set up properly, and therefore we lose some pre-existing ideas in order to make room for new material. Buzz suiting up in the locker room, getting briefed by Díaz, and climbing into the XL-15 are a few of those older elements I boarded that served as tentpole moments for this sequence. Nicolle Castro jumped on to board the new material that would help maximize the entertainment as well as elevate the stakes of Buzz's mission. **DEAN KELLY, Story Supervisor**

This marks a momentous occasion as Buzz is set to test out the new fuel crystal in a mission that will put his life on the line. He is hopeful and firmly believes that this will finally fix the mistake he made—that he will bring everyone home and return his own life and Alisha's back to normal where they can be Space Rangers again. **NICOLLE CASTRO, Story Artist**

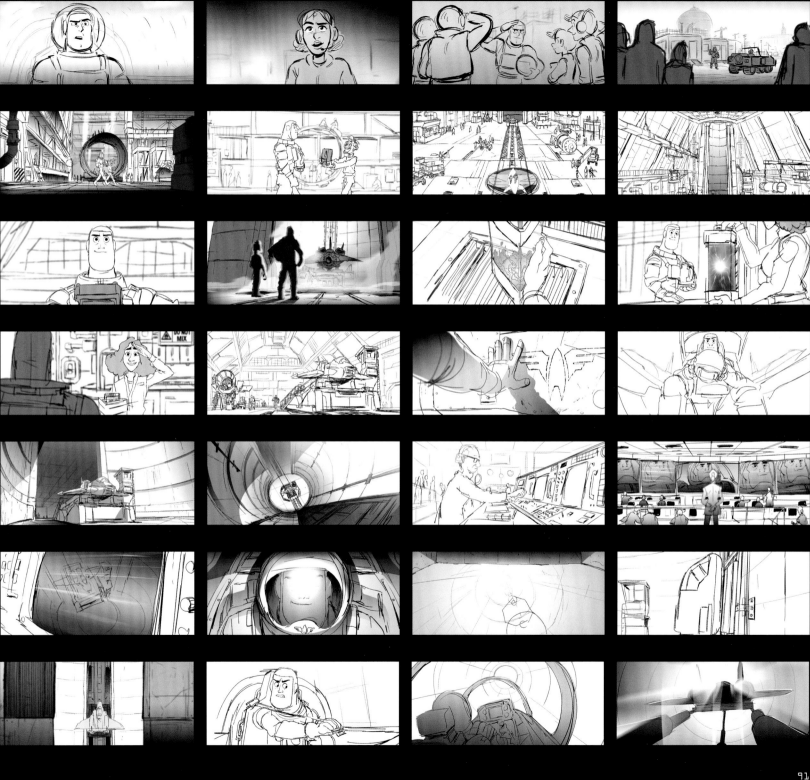

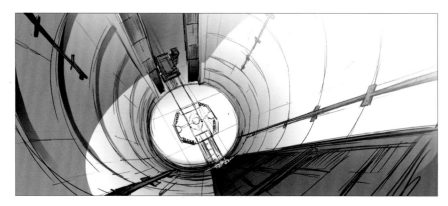

DEAN KELLY, digital

GREG PELTZ, digital

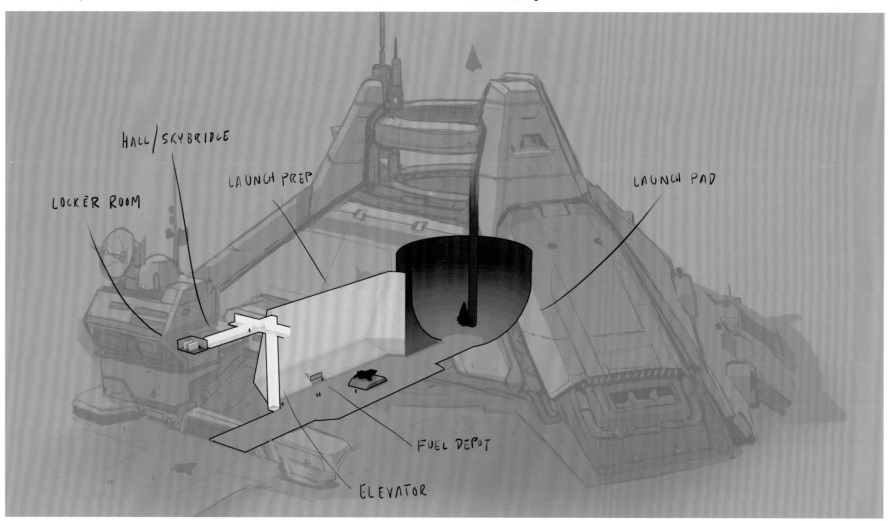

HALL/SKYBRIDGE

LAUNCH PREP

LOCKER ROOM

LAUNCH PAD

FUEL DEPOT

ELEVATOR

ABOVE AND OPPOSITE GREG PELTZ, digital

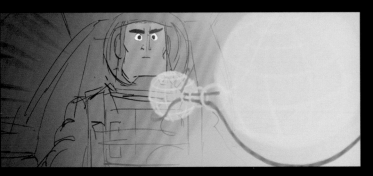

DEAN KELLY, digital

NATHAN FARRIS, digital model

NATHAN FARRIS (model); THOMAS JORDAN (shading): digital

TIM EVATT, digital

NATHAN FARRIS (model);
THOMAS JORDAN (shading): digital

The holograms needed to convey a dense amount of information while still fitting into *Lightyear*'s retro-tech aesthetic. The look is a throwback to the films that inspired us as kids and how they imagined what the future might look like. Nearly all departments were involved as graphic designers, modelers, shaders, animators, lighters, and compositors worked together to execute IVAN's flight plan.

IAN MEGIBBEN, Director of Photography, Lighting

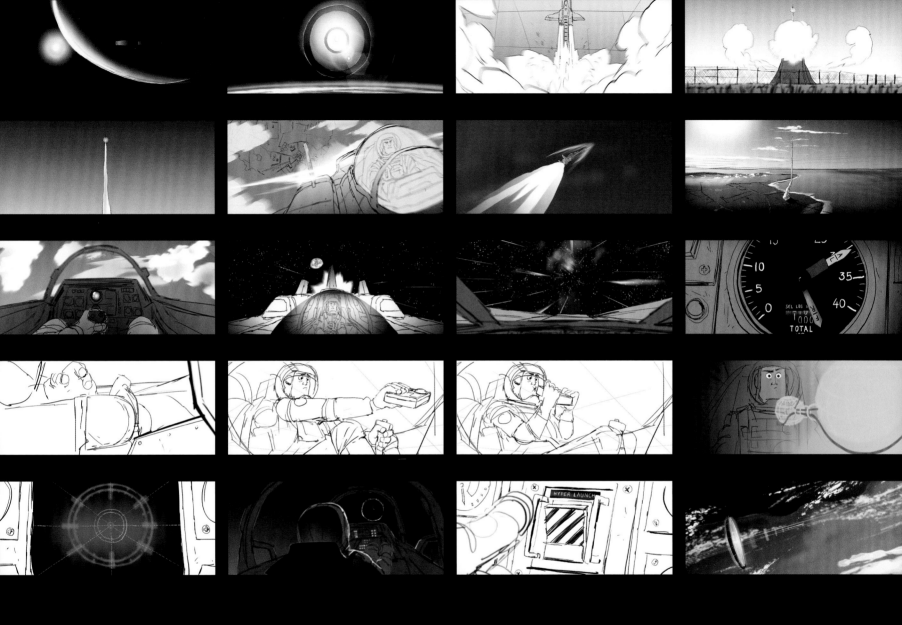

FIRST MISSION

DEAN KELLY, digital

This was the first *Lightyear* sequence I boarded back in the beginning of 2018. Angus and I sat down early on and talked about films he frequently draws inspiration from and his filmmaking likes and dislikes. From those conversations, I knew the tone he wanted to strike with this sequence. Angus gave me the freedom to visually explore so much in this sequence, with specific focus on my shot composition and exploring the scale, speed, and depth of space. The main story point was to cinematically showcase just how dangerous these lightspeed missions are. Through action we were able to further define Buzz's character and what he's willing to risk to finish his mission. **DEAN KELLY, Story Supervisor**

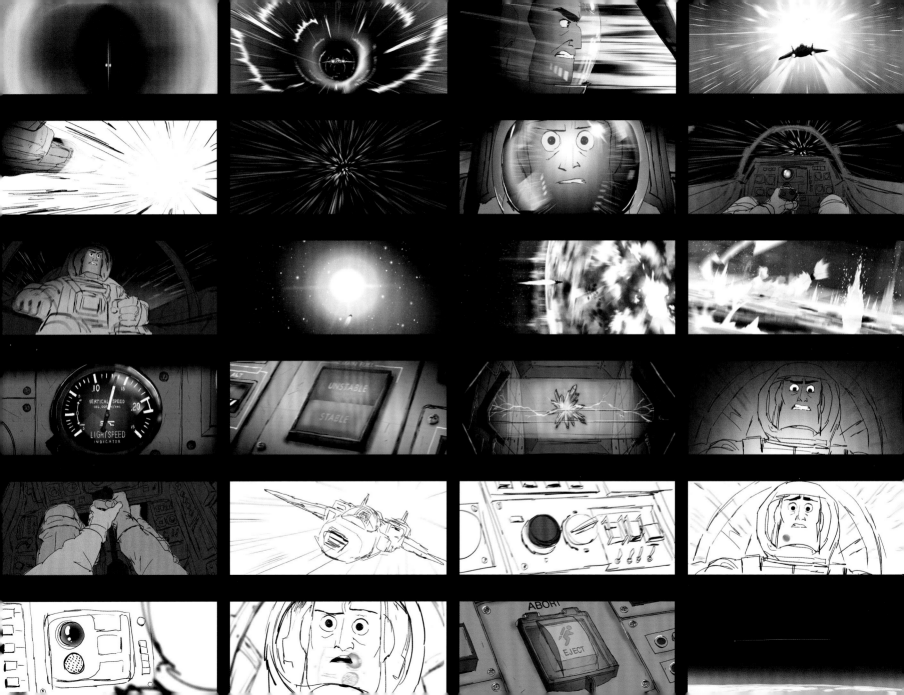

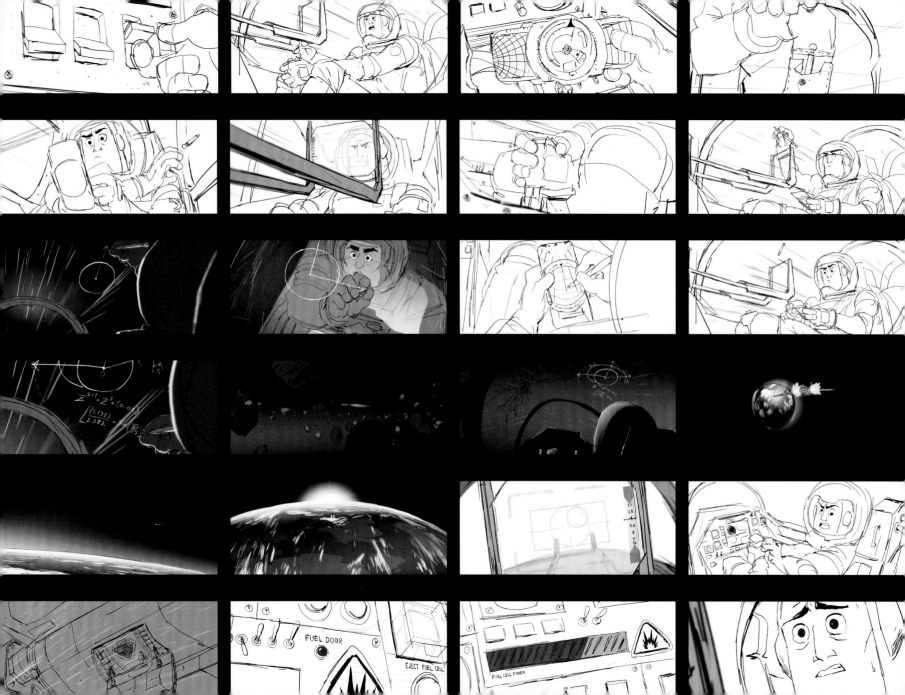

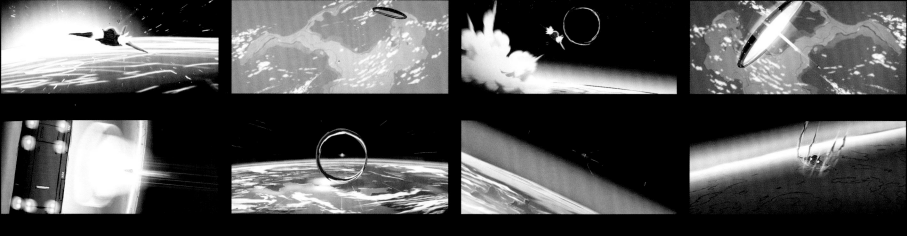

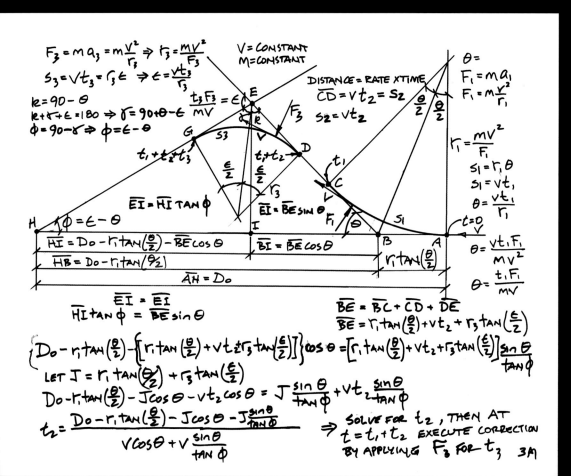

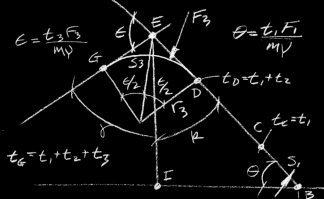

We needed a math equation for Buzz to write out on the canopy in the first hyper-speed test mission. My father is a retired mechanical engineer, and I asked him what the math would look like for a spaceship looking to correct its trajectory using an explosive device. A week later he sent me these equations. For the purposes of the movie we had to drastically reduce the amount of math featured on the canopy, but in the spirit of "showing your work," here is the complete equation on the left and the screen-used version on the right.

ANGUS MacLANE, Director

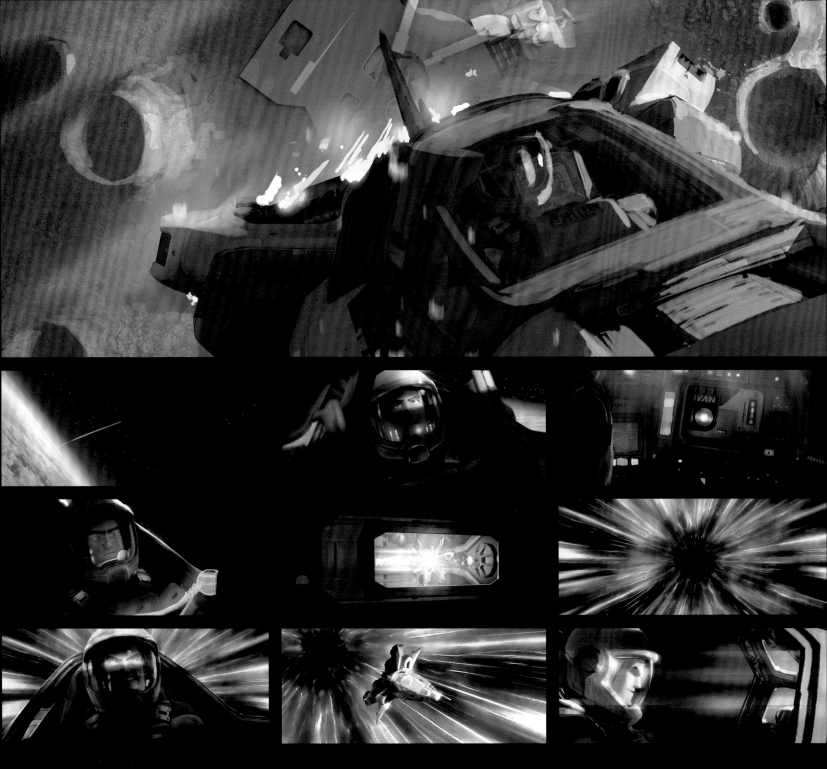

THIS SPREAD TIM EVATT, digital

103

The planet of T'Kani Prime is the primary location of our film. It had to be a somewhat hostile planet where the Star Command crew would not want to settle. We decided to give the planet a cratered look, as if before developing an atmosphere the landscape was marred by the impact of incoming meteorites. We kept the landscape mostly free of vegetation, except for some high trees, and decided that geothermal activity added to the steamy, noxious look. This gave the planet the desolate, otherworldly feel which the story required.

GARRETT TAYLOR, Sets Art Director

GARRETT TAYLOR, digital

RANDY BERRETT, digital

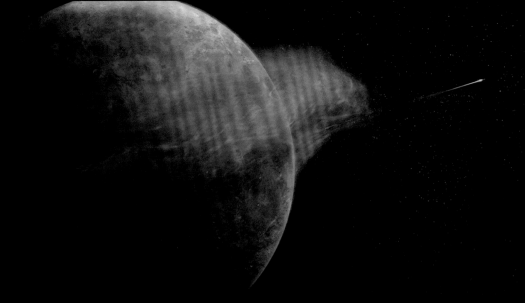

BILL ZAHN, digital

GARRETT TAYLOR, digital

ANGUS MacLANE, LEGO® bricks;
DEBORAH COLEMAN, photography

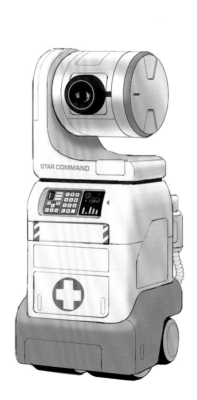

GRANT ALEXANDER, digital

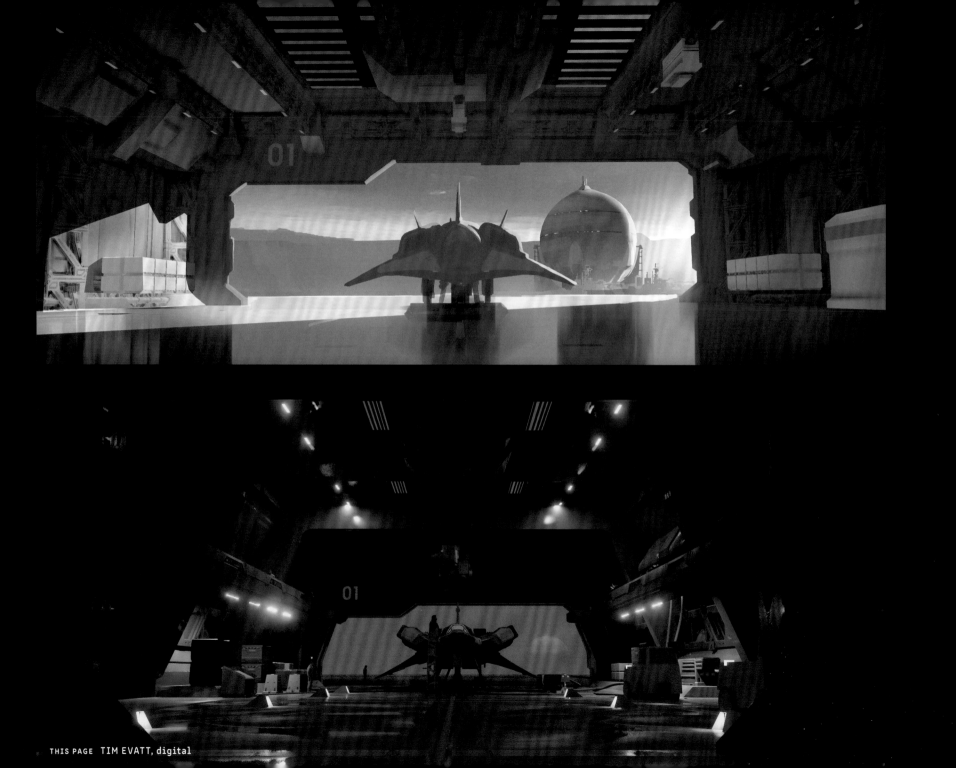

THIS PAGE TIM EVATT, digital

DEAN KELLY, digital

DEAN KELLY, digital

TIM EVATT, digital

GARRETT TAYLOR, digital

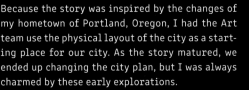

Because the story was inspired by the changes of my hometown of Portland, Oregon, I had the Art team use the physical layout of the city as a starting place for our city. As the story matured, we ended up changing the city plan, but I was always charmed by these early explorations.

ANGUS MacLANE, Director

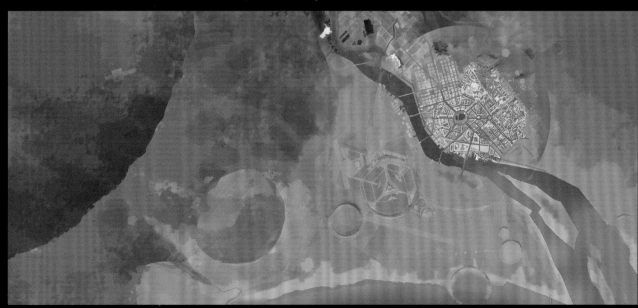

RIGHT **GARRETT TAYLOR, digital**

Work in progress! Work in progress!

Work in progress! Work in progress!

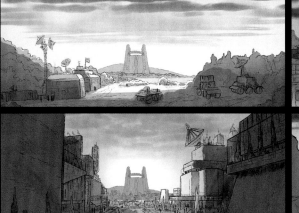

In order to create this feeling of the passage of time, I had to imagine generations of peoples' lives behind every landscape and background design I was imagining—like I was a kid playing with LEGO® bricks. Then I had to project how nature would come back over it. It was a very deep meditative exercise.

MELODY CISINSKI, Story Artist

ABOVE JOSHUA VIERS, digital

LEFT MELODY CISINSKI, digital

MELODY CISINSKI, digital

GARRETT TAYLOR, digital

IAN MEGIBBEN, digital

TIM EVATT, digital

CHEN ZHANG (model); TRENT CROW (shading): digital

IAN MEGIBBEN, digital

GARRETT TAYLOR, digital

GREG PELTZ (3D model);
BEN BEECH (shading): digital

GOING AGAIN

JEFF CALL, digital

Montages are movie moments that contrast stasis and change. In this case, we show that Buzz's missions keep failing over and over and the coffee stays bad (stasis), while Buzz's dearest friend Alisha grows older and Buzz's frustration mounts (change). My challenge was to make this contrast entertaining and something that would jump out to the audience. **JEFF CALL, Story Artist**

TIM EVATT, digital

PAUL TOPOLOS,
digital shading

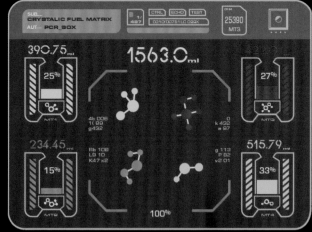

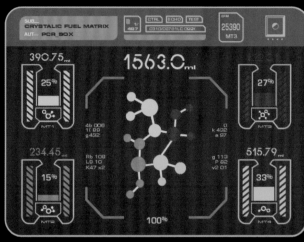

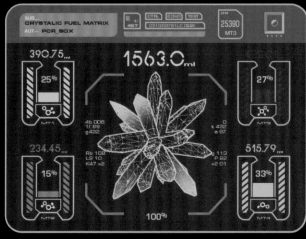

PAUL CONRAD, (graphic design); ANDY JIMENEZ
(motion graphics): digital

THIS SPREAD TIM EVATT and IAN MEGIBBEN, digital

THIS PAGE GARETT TAYLOR, digital

THIS PAGE MELODY CISINSKI, digital

OLD IZZY

NICOLLE CASTRO, digital

Right after Buzz travels to the future, he serendipitously meets Alisha's granddaughter Izzy, who has grown up to be a strong, driven, and heroic person much like himself. It was a treat to set up the dynamic between the two of them; both

start to have expectations of each other. From his first impression of Izzy, Buzz can't help but expect her to be like Alisha, and he instantly places so much hope and confidence in her

NICOLLE CASTRO, Story Artist

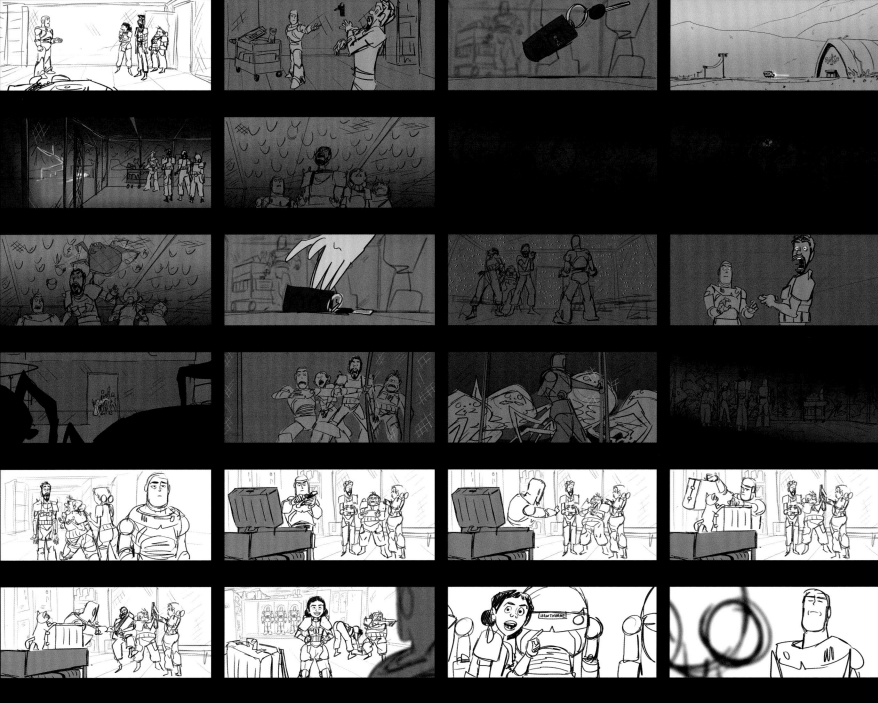

BUG'S DEATH
MARGARET SPENCER, digital

This sequence highlighted the lack of synergy in the group, and it was fun to board an increasingly frustrated Buzz on the brink of losing his patience. Setting up the threat of the hibernating bugs required striking a balance between tension and fun—an uncoordinated group dynamic made for plenty of both.
MARGARET SPENCER, Story Artist

RANDY BERRETT, digital

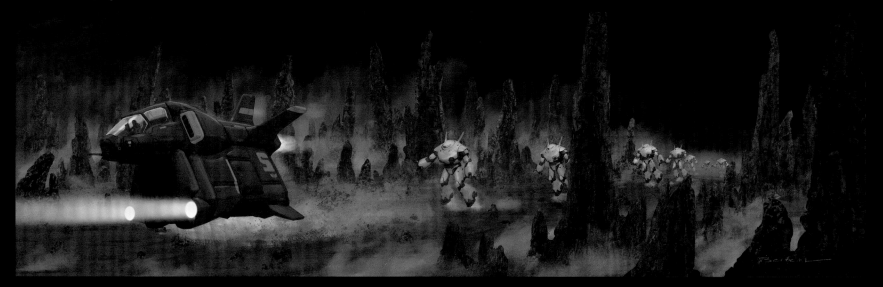

RANDY BERRETT, digital

DEAN KELLY, digital

RANDY BERRETT, digital

DEAN KELLY, digital

GARETT TAYLOR, digital

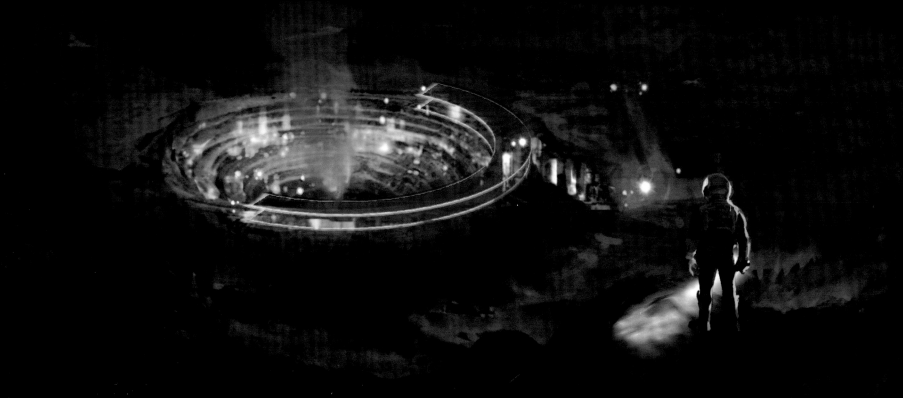

RANDY BERRETT, digital

RANDY BERRETT, digital

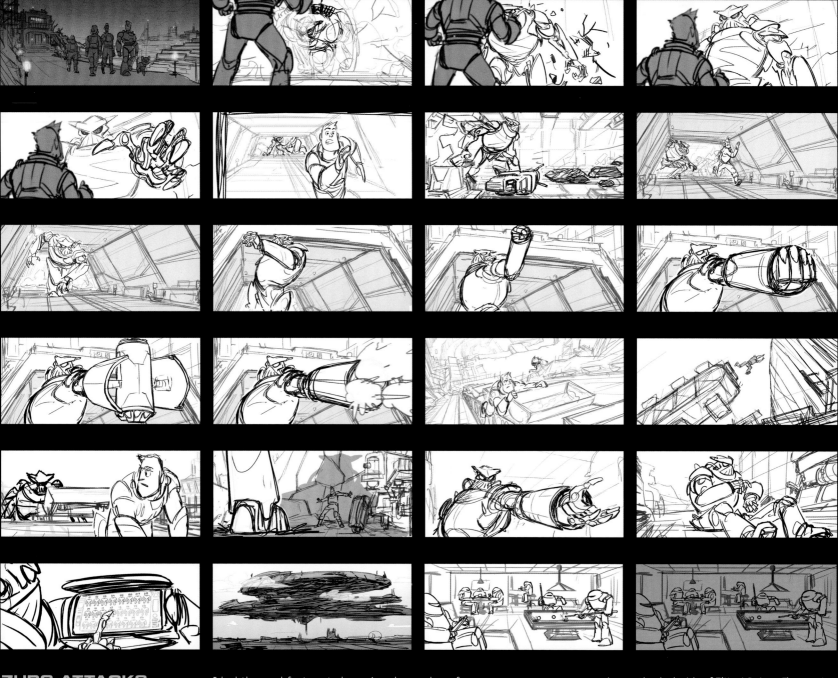

ZURG ATTACKS

DEREK THOMPSON, digital

I had the good fortune to be assigned a number of sequences involving Zurg, and this one was the most complex and challenging of them all. An earlier variation of this sequence played out in a vertical elevator shaft and later was reconceived to be set in a massive shipyard. This final iteration shifted the action to an enormous mine on the dark side of T'Kani Prime. The staging challenge was to push the chase from a horizontal orientation to a vertical one. Drawing Zurg was one of the highlights of the movie for me, and this sequence gave me a chance to showcase him in all of his glory. **DEREK THOMPSON, Story Artist**

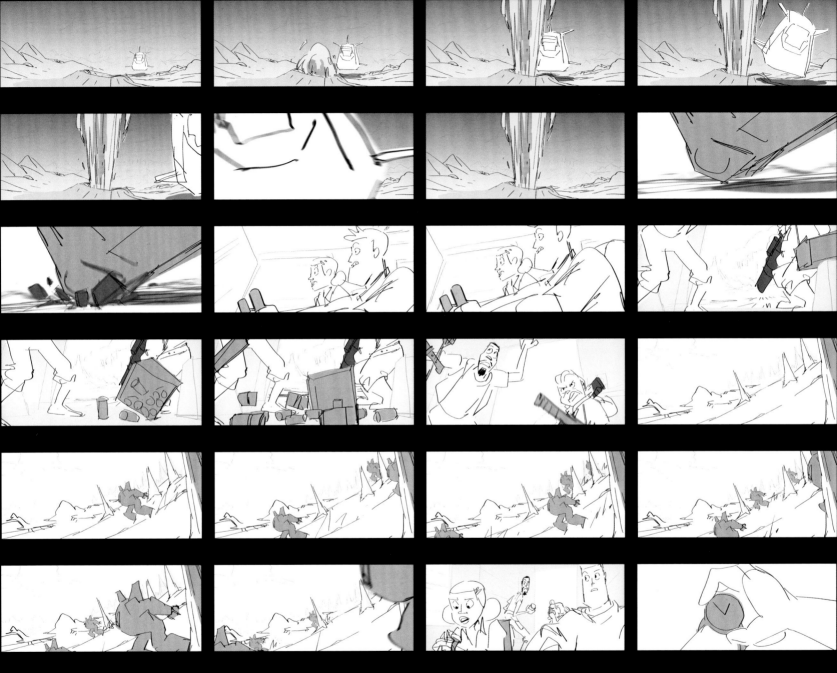

ESCAPE

MICHAEL FONG, digital

Working on a chase scene can be really difficult, but a good chase has so much potential for tension and excitement. I love vehicles and mechs in movies and animation, so this was a fun challenge to try to make this scene as cool as possible. I looked at a lot of car chase and racing scenes for inspiration because the gang was originally driving Darby's bug extermination van. In a later version, the van changed to the Armadillo ship, but by then the scene was so huge it took everyone on the story team to help swap the van for the Armadillo.
MICHAEL FONG, Story Artist

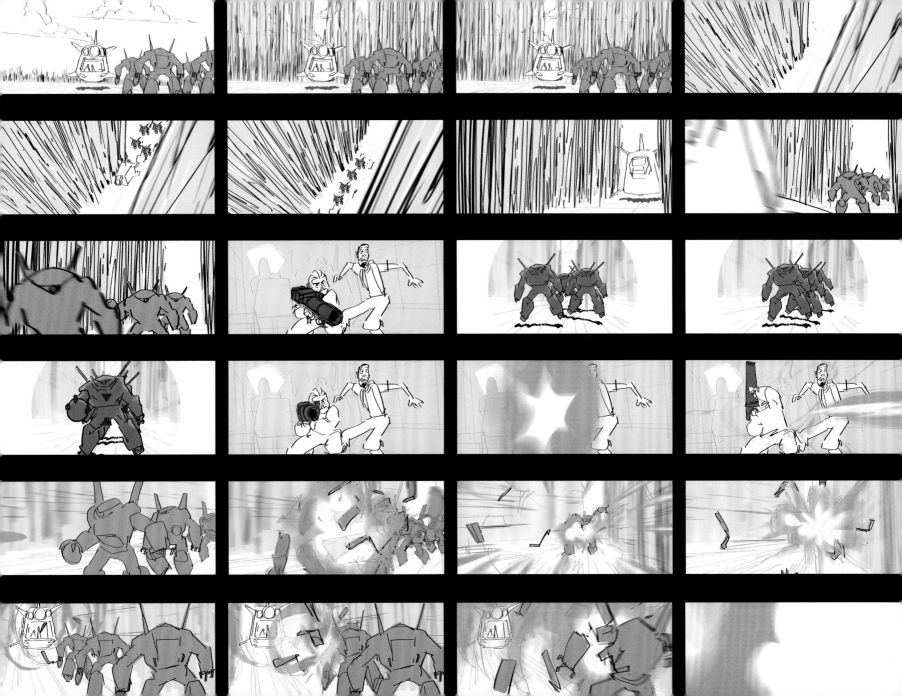

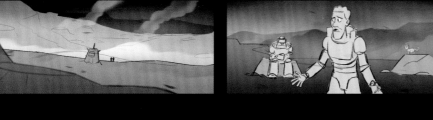
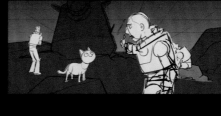

STRANDED   CHARLES CHOO JR., digital

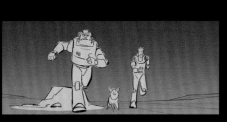
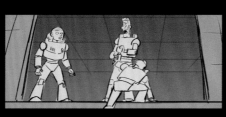

TO SPACE
CHARLES CHOO JR., digital

This scene comes after the team's low point where all hope seems lost. The team is thinking of a way out, when Izzy finds a teleportation disc on the ship that would allow them to teleport to Zurg's ship, giving them a chance to get back with Buzz. **CHARLES CHOO JR., Story Artist**

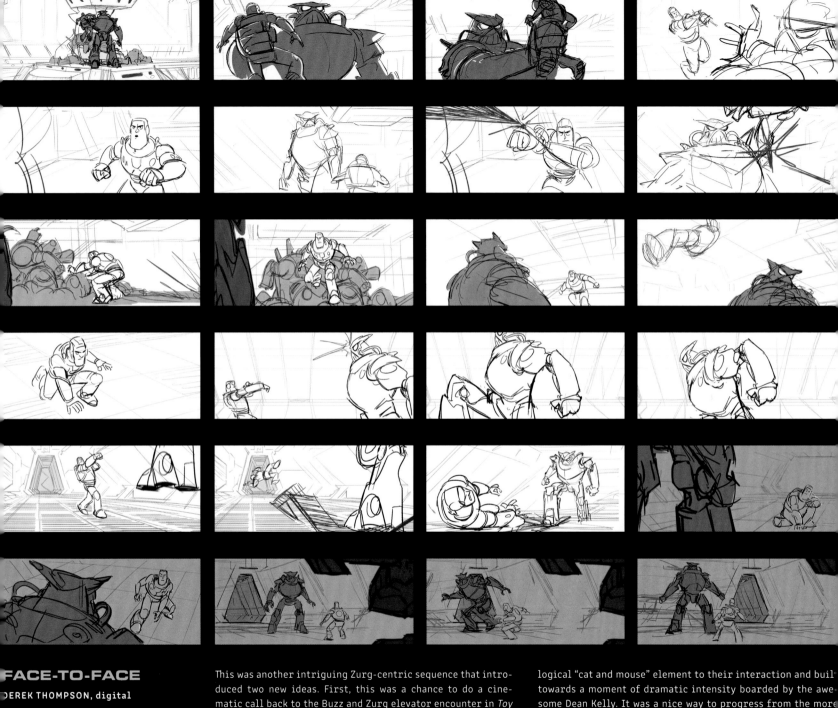

FACE-TO-FACE

DEREK THOMPSON, digital

This was another intriguing Zurg-centric sequence that intro-
duced two new ideas. First, this was a chance to do a cinematic call back to the Buzz and Zurg elevator encounter in *Toy
Story 2*, and I used explicit setups to connect to the original

logical "cat and mouse" element to their interaction and buil
towards a moment of dramatic intensity boarded by the awe
some Dean Kelly. It was a nice way to progress from the more
visceral and action driven Zurg scenes I'd boarded earlier in

We wanted the design of the Zurg environments to be distinct from those of Star Command. The manufactured design of Star Command has a warm, rounded feel with right angles and asymmetrical details. The Zurg world, in contrast, is robotically symmetrical and features oblique angles and repeated design details. The former is a human world, with all of the warmth of such, where the latter is a technologically cold and alien one.

GARRETT TAYLOR, Sets Art Director

GARRETT TAYLOR, digital

GARRETT TAYLOR, digital

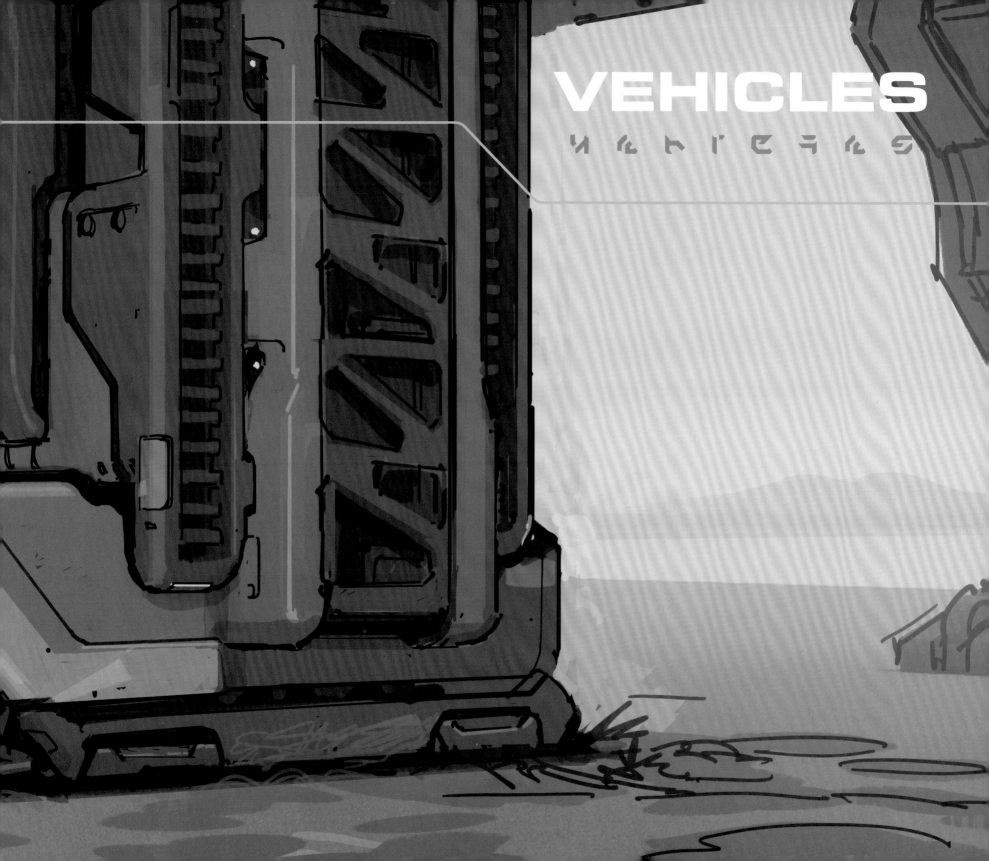

VEHICLES

DEAN KELLY, digital

ANGUS MacLANE, digital

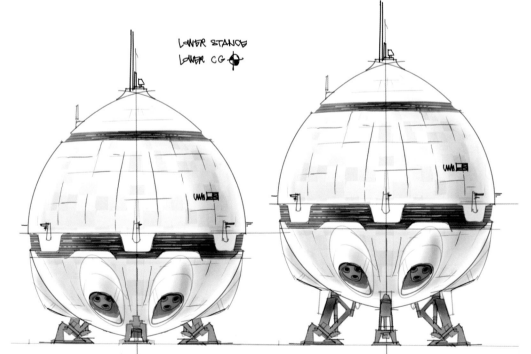

JAY SHUSTER, digital

GARETT TAYLOR, digital

GARRETT TAYLOR, digital

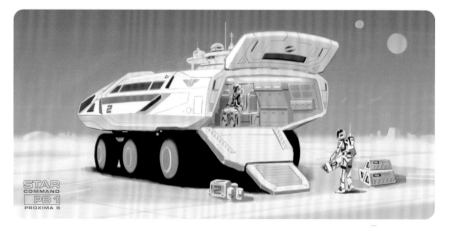

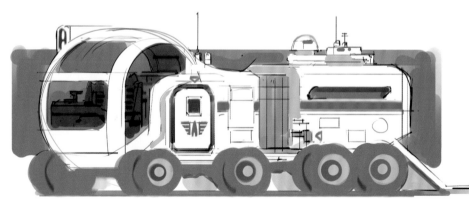

THIS PAGE GRANT ALEXANDER, digital

GRANT ALEXANDER, digital

GRANT ALEXANDER, digital

DEAN KELLY, digital

LEGS ARE ORNAMENTAL

HOMEMADE FIBERGLASS INSECT ON TOP OF TRUCK

DEAN KELLY, pencil

ANGUS MacLANE, LEGO® bricks; DEBORAH COLEMAN, photography

GARRETT TAYLOR, digital

ANGUS MacLANE, LEGO® bricks; DEBORAH COLEMAN, photography

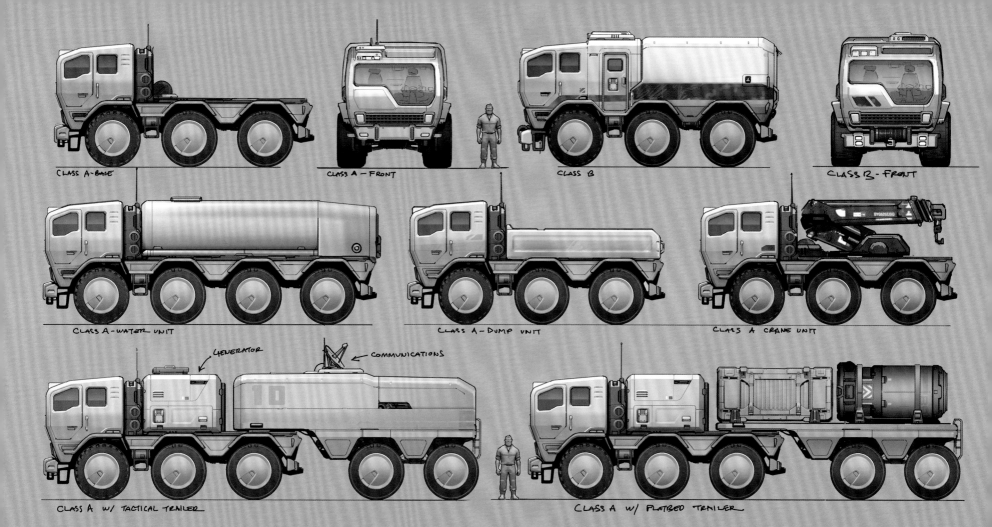

CLASS A-BASE

CLASS A – FRONT

CLASS B

CLASS B – FRONT

CLASS A – WATER UNIT

CLASS A – DUMP UNIT

CLASS A CRANE UNIT

GENERATOR

COMMUNICATIONS

CLASS A W/ TACTICAL TRAILER

CLASS A W/ FLATBED TRAILER

RACK

SNORKLE

CLASS C FRONT

STAR COMMAND
ROVER DEPLOYMENTS

THIS PAGE GARRETT TAYLOR, digital

CLASS A ROVER

WITH TACTICAL TRAILER

LEGO® building is a hobby that I enjoy mostly because it provides a meditative escape from digital film production. It's an artistic medium that allows for quick prototyping, and I used LEGO builds to brainstorm the designs for many of the film's vehicles. I would work out the shapes in a quick LEGO model and then show it to the Art team who would take these rough sketches, detail them out, and align them to the world of the film. In the end, one of my ERIC robot designs was incorporated into one of the official LEGO sets released for the film.

ANGUS MacLANE, Director

ANGUS MacLANE, LEGO® bricks and photography

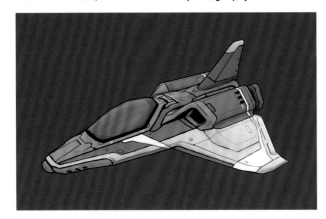

GREG PELTZ, digital

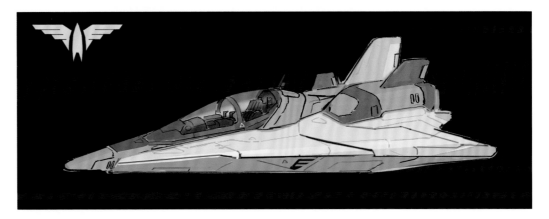

GRANT ALEXANDER, digital

TIM EVATT, photography

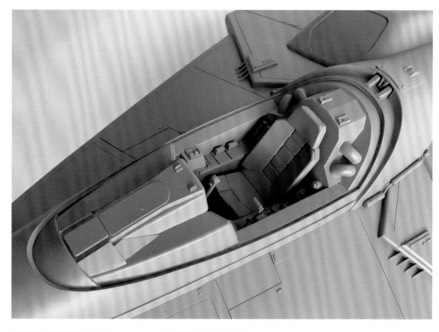

JOHN DUNCAN, fabricated model; TIM EVATT, photography

Maintaining the charm of our vehicle and architecture drawings in their translation to 3D was huge for us. Avoiding simple, flat shapes while embracing lots of rounds, radiuses, and bevels gave our models a sculptural quality that was appealing, chunky, and fun.

GREG PELTZ, Sets Art Director

JOHN DUNCAN, fabricated model;
TIM EVATT, photography

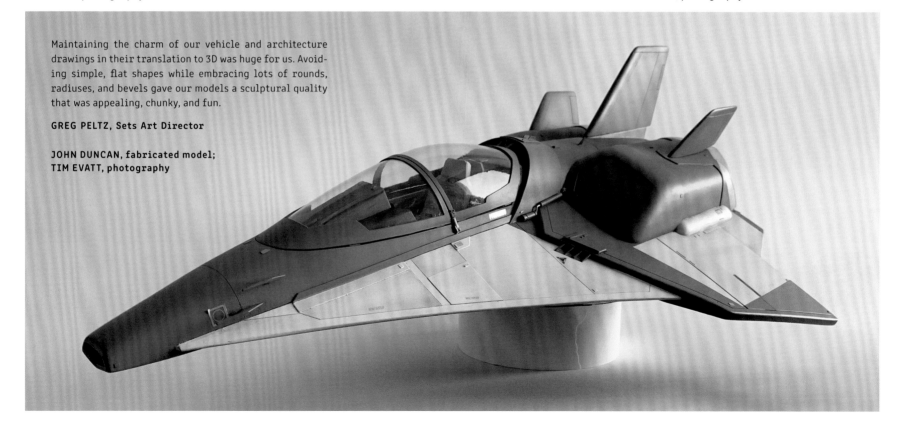

There is something about holding a physical model in your hands that allows you to easily envision its role in its world. You can see the light glints and shadows, the surface texture and negative space—it makes it real! Angus and Tim's designs draw from sci-fi but are also grounded with contemporary aircraft elements that lend a level of believability in the design. The ship was made using traditional model making techniques like vacuum-forming with kit-bashing for details.

JOHN DUNCAN, Development Artist

THIS PAGE JOHN DUNCAN, fabricated model; TIM EVATT, photography

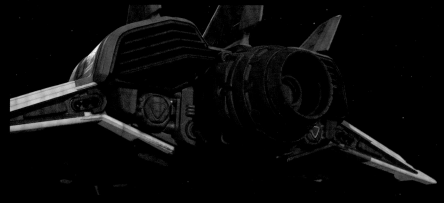

XL-01 OVERVIEW

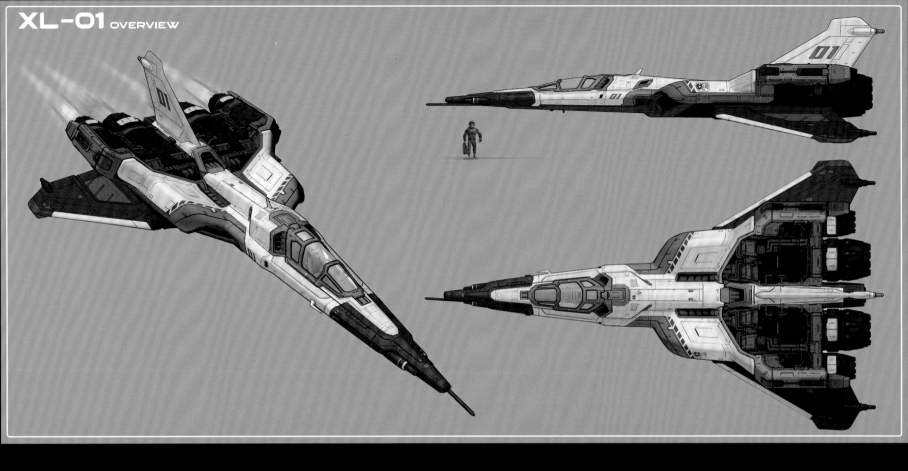

XL-01 ENGINES

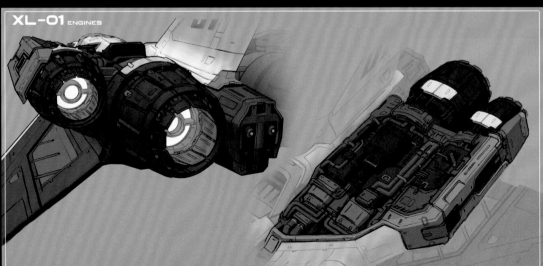

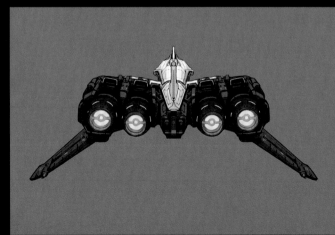

THIS SPREAD GREG PELTZ, digital

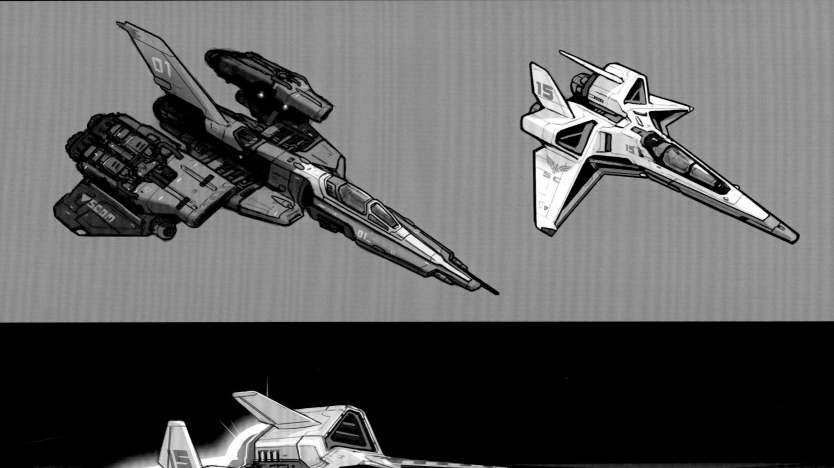
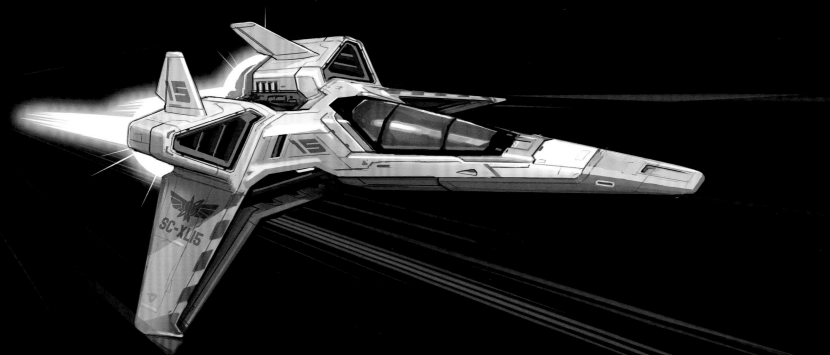

THIS PAGE GREG PELTZ (model); BEN BEECH (shading): digital

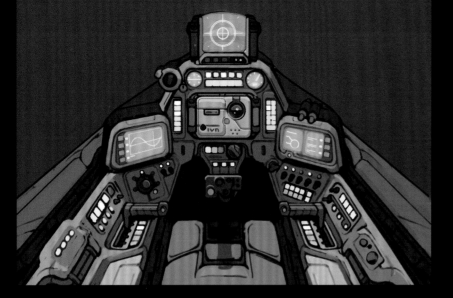

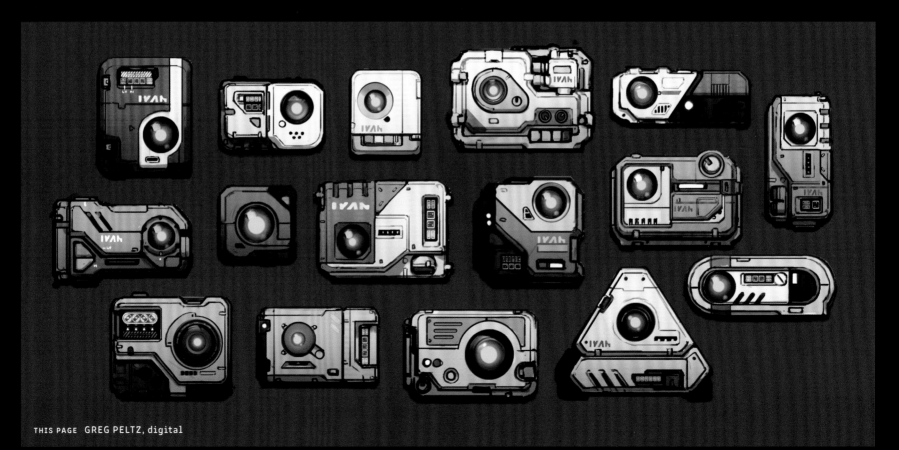

THIS PAGE GREG PELTZ, digital

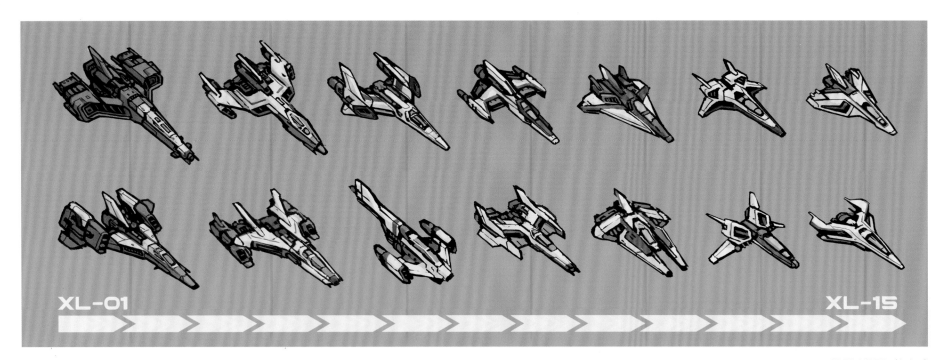

XL-01

XL-15

GREG PELTZ, digital

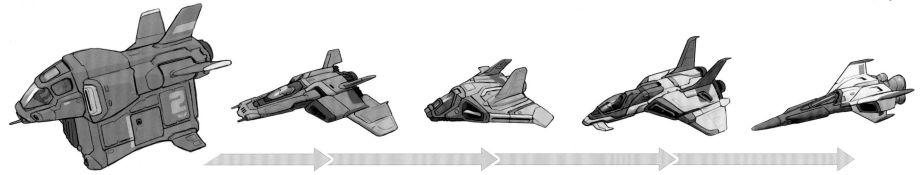

GREG PELTZ, digital

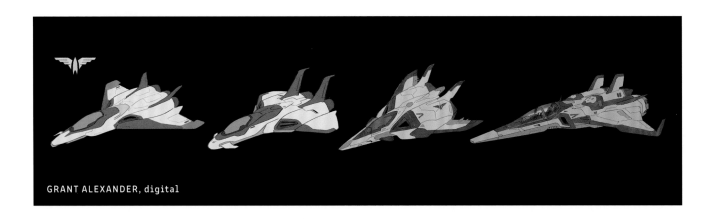

GRANT ALEXANDER, digital

As the ships progress over the passage of time, we wanted to distinguish each one not only through color but material changes as well. At the start of the film, the XL-01 has a rougher, more matte finish with a lot of exposed metal and pipes. By the time we reach the XL-15, the ships have a glossier paint finish with sleeker, more refined metals.

BEN BEECH, Lead Technical Director

ANGUS MacLANE, LEGO® bricks; DEBORAH COLEMAN, photography

GREG PELTZ, digital

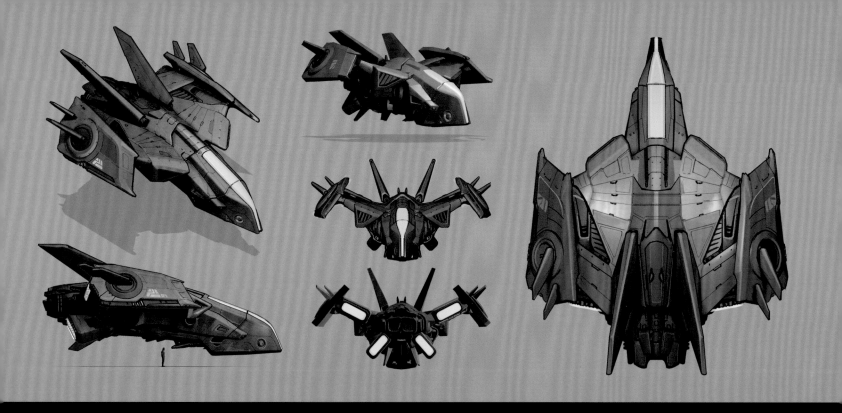

GARRETT TAYLOR, digital

JOSH WEST, model; PAUL TOPOLOS, shading, digital

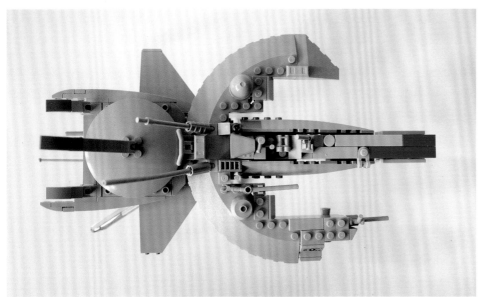

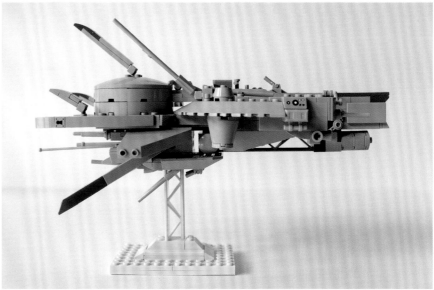

ANGUS MacLANE, LEGO® bricks; DEBORAH COLEMAN, photography

TIM EVATT, gouache

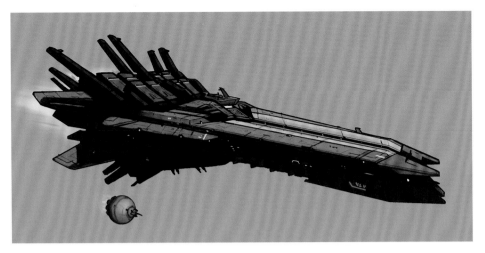

GREG PELTZ, digital

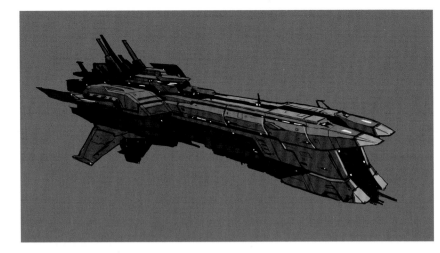

GREG PELTZ, digital

GARRETT TAYLOR, digital

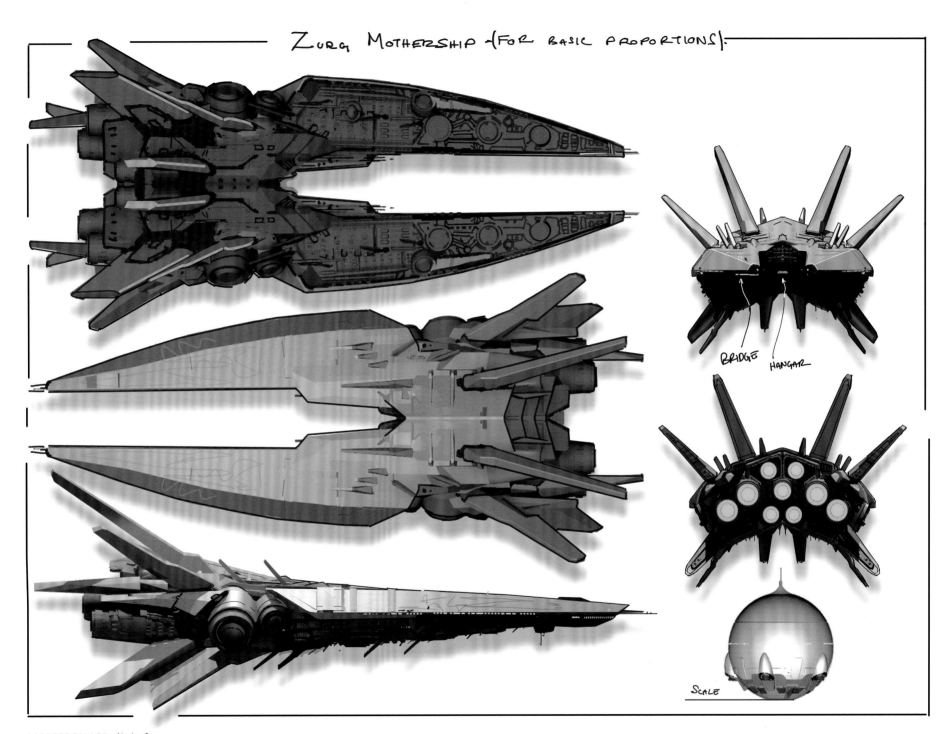

Zurg Mothership (for basic proportions)

BRIDGE HANGAR

SCALE

GARRETT TAYLOR, digital

155

LIGHTYEAR NEEDS TO WORK IN BLACK AND WHITE

GARRETT TAYLOR and TIM EVATT, digital

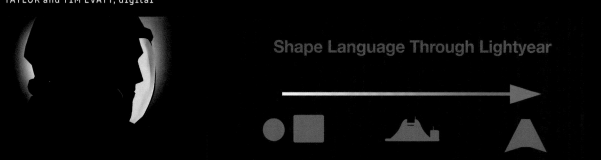

Shape Language Through Lightyear

Lightyear had a lot to track because of the time travel aspect of the film. We needed to know what state our colony was in at what time of the movie. The colony needed to evolve/progress as time passed. For inspiration, we looked at the NASA logo and its progression through time. We asked ourselves how this logo design progression could be extrapolated into a visual design to influence our colony as it too evolved.

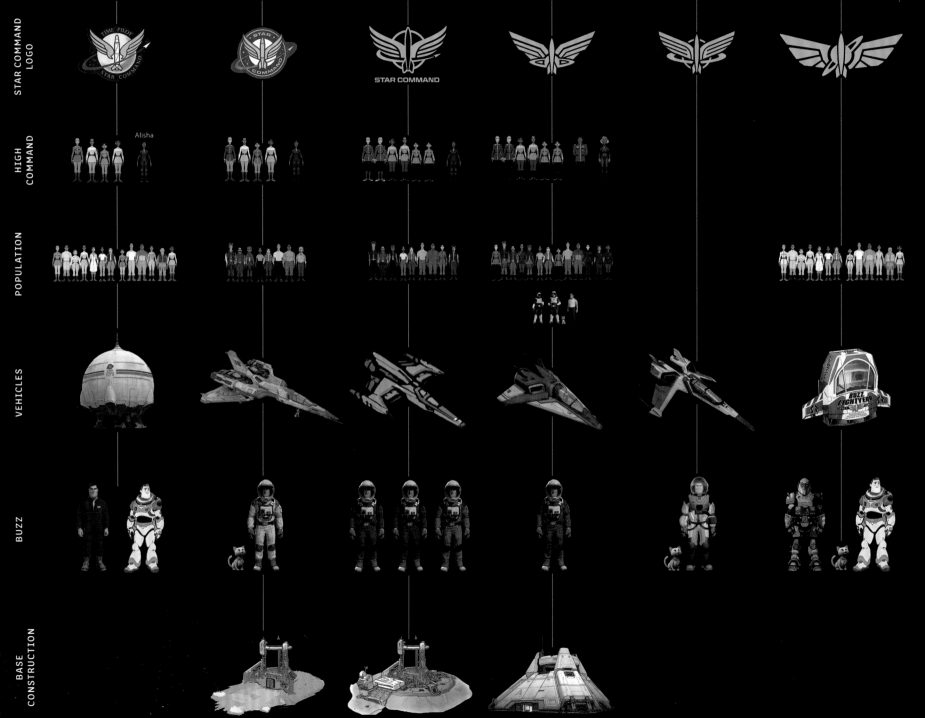

STAR COMMAND LOGO

HIGH COMMAND

Alisha

POPULATION

VEHICLES

BUZZ

BASE CONSTRUCTION

BUZZ ENVIRONMENT
STYLE NOTES

THIS IS A SET OF NOTES FOR THE ART DIRECTION OF ALL STAR COMMAND RELATED ENVIRONMENTS. IT IS A SET OF DESIGN "RULES." WE WILL WANT TO BREAK THESE RULES AS NECESSARY TO SUPPORT THE STORY WITH PURPOSEFUL DESIGN DECISIONS. BUT THE ARTISTS SHOULD AT LEAST HAVE THESE IN MIND.

ASYMMETRICAL DESIGN

USED   CEMENT   HUMAN   ANALOG

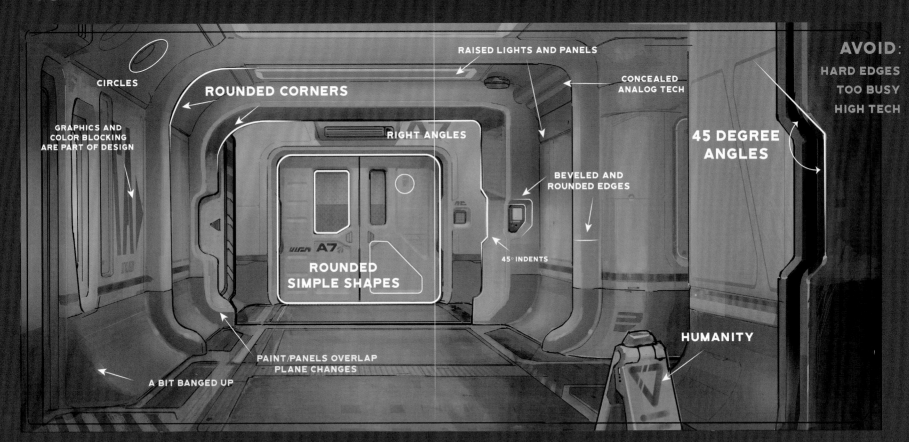

CIRCLES

GRAPHICS AND COLOR BLOCKING ARE PART OF DESIGN

ROUNDED CORNERS

RAISED LIGHTS AND PANELS

CONCEALED ANALOG TECH

RIGHT ANGLES

AVOID:
HARD EDGES
TOO BUSY
HIGH TECH

45 DEGREE ANGLES

BEVELED AND ROUNDED EDGES

ROUNDED SIMPLE SHAPES

ULGA A7

45° INDENTS

HUMANITY

PAINT/PANELS OVERLAP PLANE CHANGES

A BIT BANGED UP

HORIZONTAL

ZURG
ENVIRONMENT
STYLE NOTES

THIS IS A SET OF NOTES FOR THE ART DIRECTION OF ALL ZURG RELATED ENVIRONMENTS. IT IS A SET OF DESIGN "RULES." WE WILL WANT TO BREAK THESE RULES AS NECESSARY TO SUPPORT THE STORY WITH PURPOSEFUL DESIGN DECISIONS. BUT THE ARTISTS SHOULD AT LEAST HAVE THESE IN MIND.

CLEAN

METAL

SYMMETRICAL DESIGN

ROBOTIC

DIGITAL

VERTICAL

SHARP SHAPES

PURPOSEFUL ASYMMETRY

AVOID:
CIRCLES
RIGHT ANGLES
PARALLEL LINES

TIGHT BEVELED EDGES

OBLIQUE ANGLES

IRREGULAR POLYGONS

EXPOSED, HIGH-FREQUENCY TECH

FLUSH LIGHTS AND PANELS

REPETITION LOOKS SPINAL

Z

STAR COMMAND

As a fan of movie and comic book space-men since childhood, creating the world of Buzz and Star Command was this designer's dream come true. Not only would I be designing all of the ship, hologram, and screen graphics, but also Star Command's overall space military "brand." The added challenge would be thinking through the ever changing looks of sets, ships, and suits due to Buzz's time jumps. This would include the SC brand and logo changes, the NASA-inspired mission patches, and a system of rank for character's promotions. Everything from spaceships to food packaging!

PAUL CONRAD, Graphics Art Director

THIS SPREAD   PAUL CONRAD, digital

COLORSCRIPT

THIS SPREAD TIM EVATT and IAN MEGIBBEN, digital

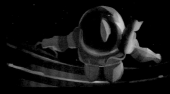

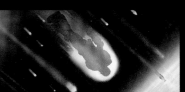

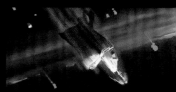

OUT OF PICTURE

CALUM ALEXANDER WATT, digital

DANIEL ARRIAGA, digital

SABINE BELOFSKY, digital

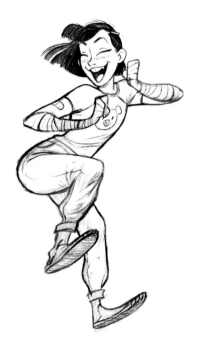

CORY LOFTIS, digital

DEAN HEEZEN, digital

CALUM ALEXANDER WATT, digital

CALUM ALEXANDER WATT, digital

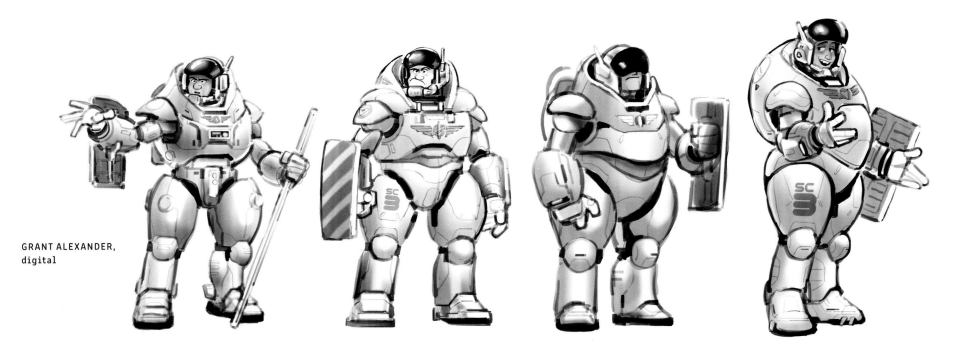

GRANT ALEXANDER,
digital

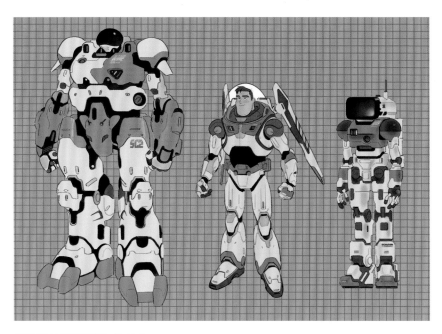

GRANT ALEXANDER, digital

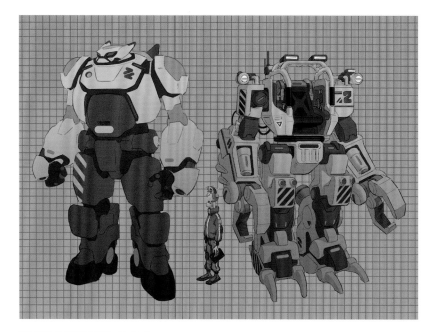

GRANT ALEXANDER, digital

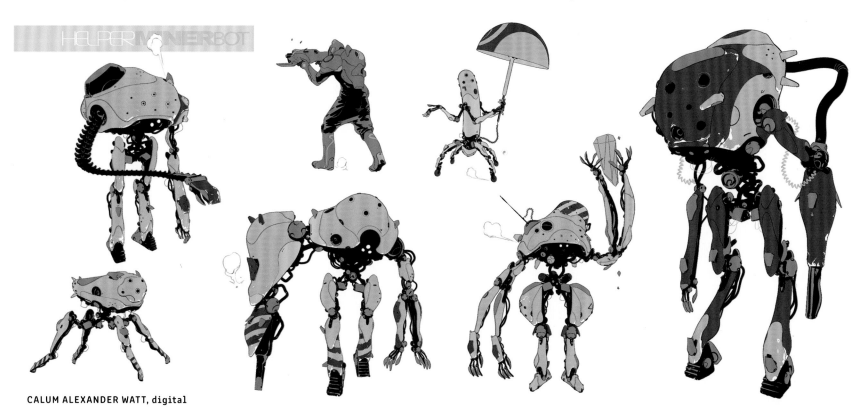

HELPER MINERBOT

CALUM ALEXANDER WATT, digital

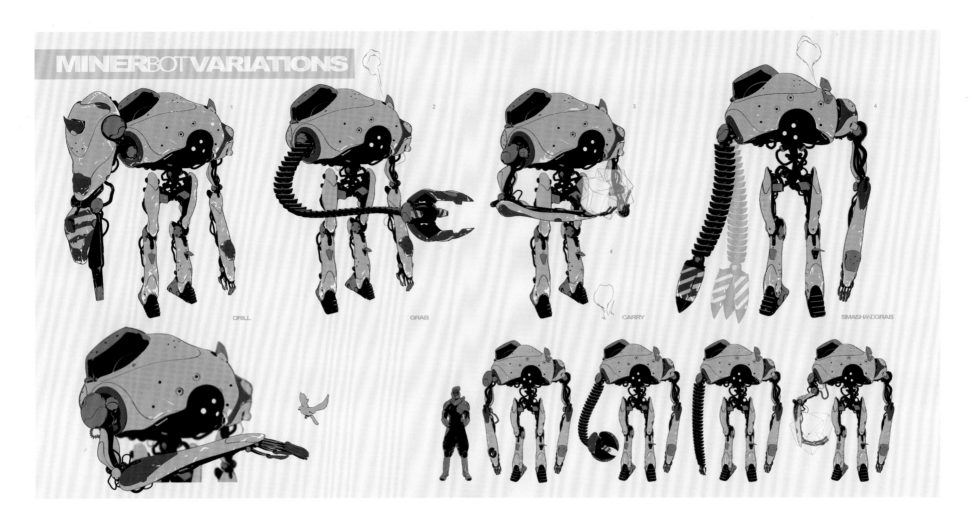

MINERBOT VARIATIONS

DRILL

GRAB

CARRY

SMASHANDGRAB

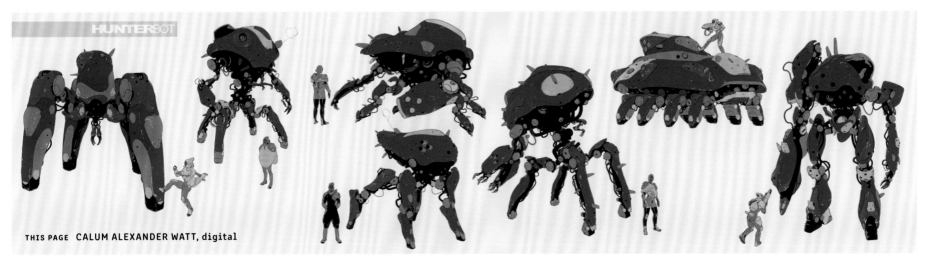

HUNTERBOT

THIS PAGE CALUM ALEXANDER WATT, digital

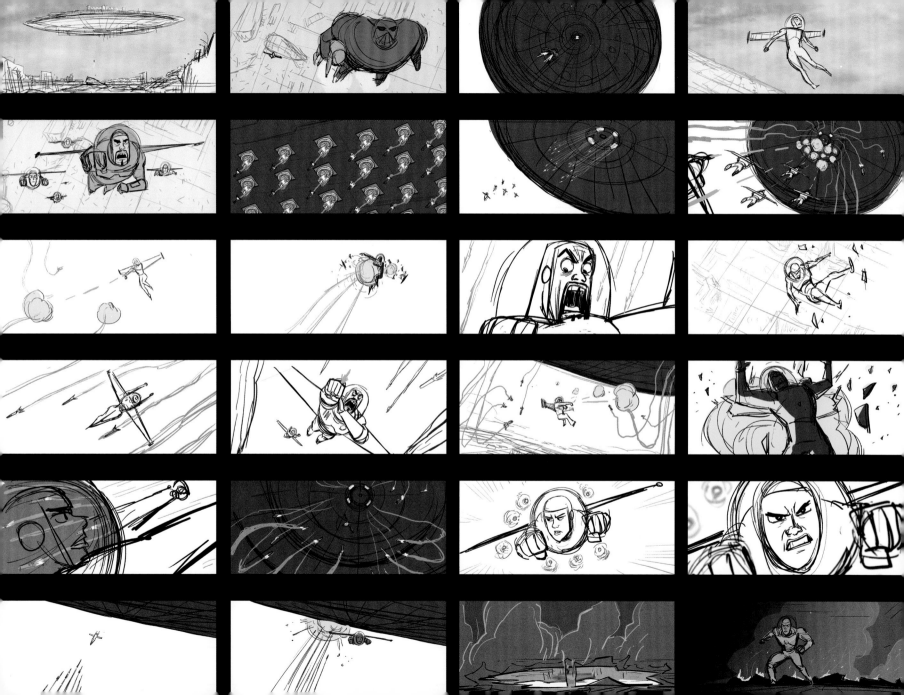

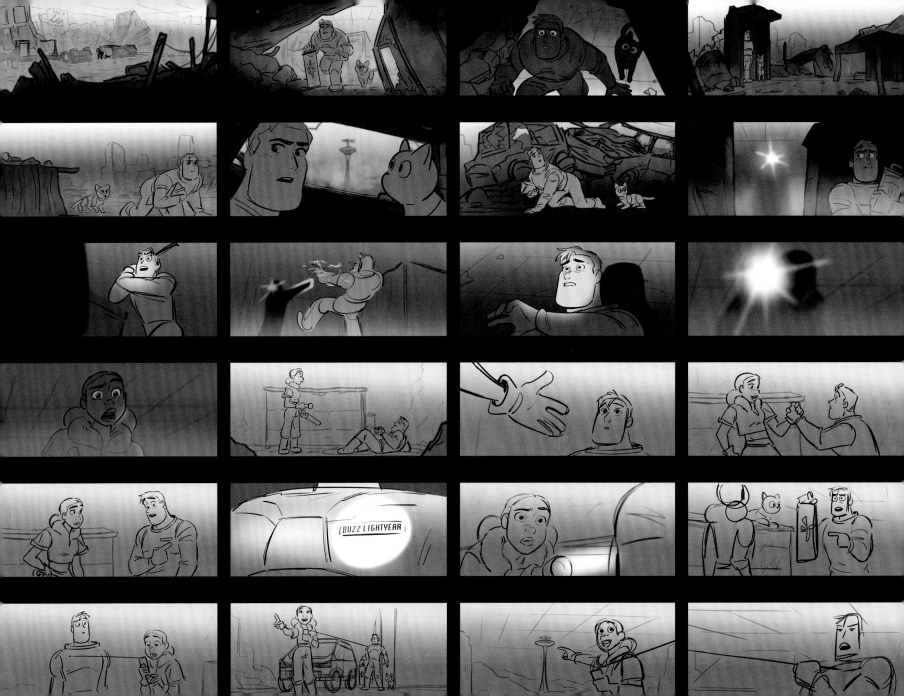

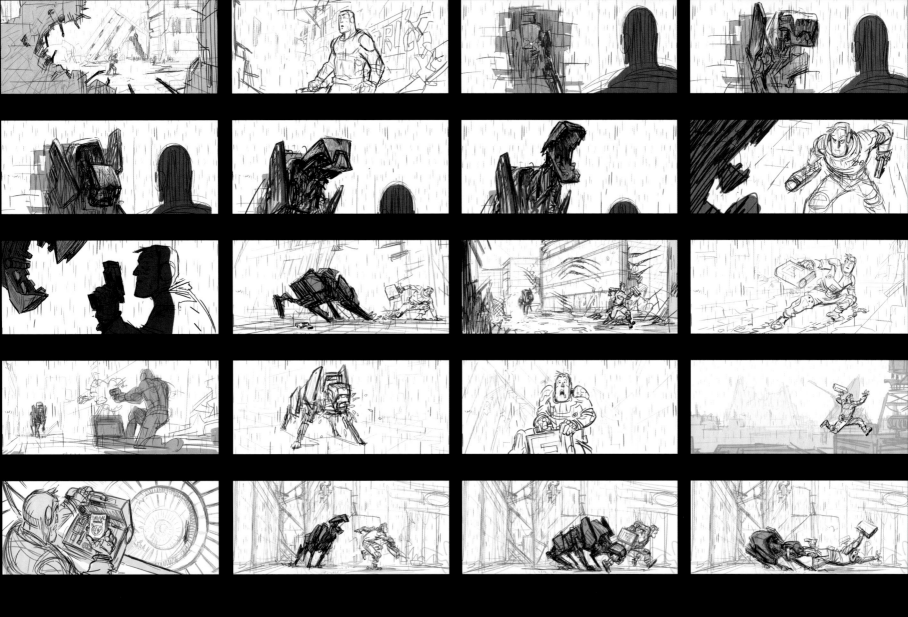

THE HOUND   DEREK THOMPSON, digital

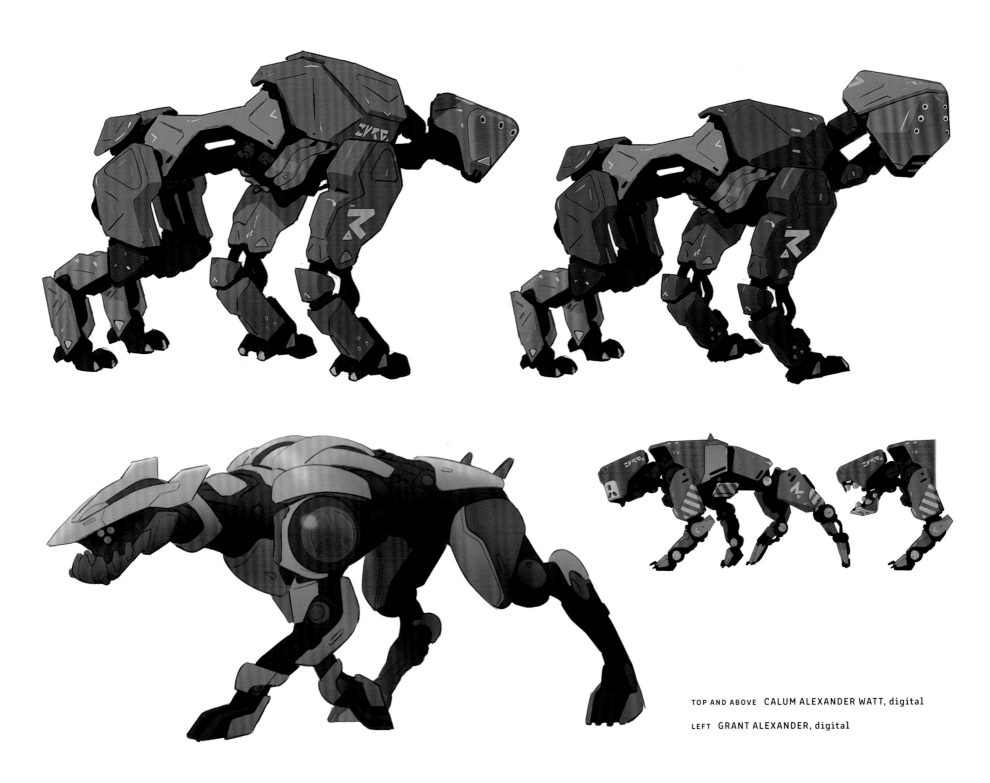

TOP AND ABOVE CALUM ALEXANDER WATT, digital

LEFT GRANT ALEXANDER, digital

ACKNOWLEDGMENTS

It is a privilege to make animated films at Pixar, as its halls are filled with some of the most talented artists in our industry. For *Lightyear* these artists faced the additional challenge of working in the isolating conditions of a global pandemic. Filmmaking is a team sport, bringing together hundreds of people to create a singular piece of art. In the best of times it requires strong vision, leadership, and collaboration. Mass quarantine challenged these skills, presenting varying unexpected hurdles that our dedicated crew managed with optimism, grace, and ingenuity.

Production Designer Tim Evatt led the collaborative charge, building an incredibly diverse and talented team of art directors and artists: Matt Nolte, Greg Peltz, Garrett Taylor, Bill Zahn, Paul Conrad, Grant Alexander, Dean Heezen, Kaleb Rice, Randy Berrett, Paul Topolos, Maria Lee, Nelson Bohol, Ben Beech, Calum Alexander Watt, John Duncan, and Joshua Viers. Ian Megibben, our Lighting Director of Photography joined Tim to create stunning and inspirational lighting keys. All of this work was made possible by the thoughtful production management of Eric Rosales, Nick Mikesell, and Jacy Johnson. Thanks to all of you for the remarkable art and vision that you brought to this film.

Our Story Team, led by the exceptionally talented Dean Kelly, created boards that not only told our story, but also conveyed all of the potential mystery and excitement of the finished product. Along with our Production Management staff of Jessica Kelly, Laura Holshouser, and Rebecca Banks and our artists represented in these pages including Bobby Alcid Rubio, Michael Fong, Derek Thompson, Margaret Spencer, Charles Choo Jr., Ted Mathot, Melody Cisinski, Sunmee Joh, Jeff Call, and Nicolle Castro. Without all of you this story would not have been told. Thank you.

Of course there would be no book without the contributions of Pixar's publishing team of Molly Jones, Jenny Moussa Spring, Deborah Cichocki, and Shiho Tilley; our Feature Relations dynamic duo of Melissa Bernabei and Maura Turner; our collaborators at Chronicle Books with Neil Egan, Liam Flanagan, Brittany McInerney, Maddy Wong, Tera Killip, Alison Petersen, and Juliette Capra; and our legal clearance team of Serena Dettman and Laura Finell. Thanks to you all for your patience and guidance through this process.

We are truly thankful for the insights of our cultural, artistic, and technical consultants, both internal and those who joined us from their various areas of expertise. A special shout out to Thomas Marshburn and all of his colleagues at NASA for opening our eyes to the science (that we mostly ignored) and the wonders (that we most definitely absorbed) of space. Warmest thanks to Major Jocelyn Flores, Cassandra Falby, Captain Tammy Binns, Dr. Mae Jemison, Rick Carter, Rachelle Federico, Andrea Goh, Fran Kalal, Chloe Kloezeman, and Sofya Ogunseitan for all of your thoughtful feedback.

NICOLLE CASTRO, "Buzz and His Apartment": digital

Our Executive Producer, Andrew Stanton, and Associate Executive Producer Emily Mollenkopf have been with us every step of the way, along with the Pixar executive team of Jim Morris, Pete Docter, Jonas Rivera, Katherine Sarafian, Tom Porter, Steve May, Britta Wilson, Jim Kennedy, Chris Kaiser, Lindsey Collins, Jonathan Garson and Reema Batnagar. We so appreciate all of your contributions and support.

I would like to thank our Director Angus MacLane for never giving up in the pursuit of excellence and our incredible crew across the entire film, led by Michael Warch, Sara Wilson, Jane Yen, and Bryan Read, who meet and continue to exceed expectations under the most challenging of circumstances.

Finally, as I sit in my home office one-and-a-half years after being sent home for our three-week COVID-19 hiatus, I must express my appreciation for all of the families who have worked with and around us, for without their support surely none of this would have been possible.

With Gratitude.

GALYN SUSMAN, PRODUCER

RIGHT NICOLLE CASTRO,
"Let's Go Find Him": digital

FATHER?!

NICOLLE CASTRO, digital

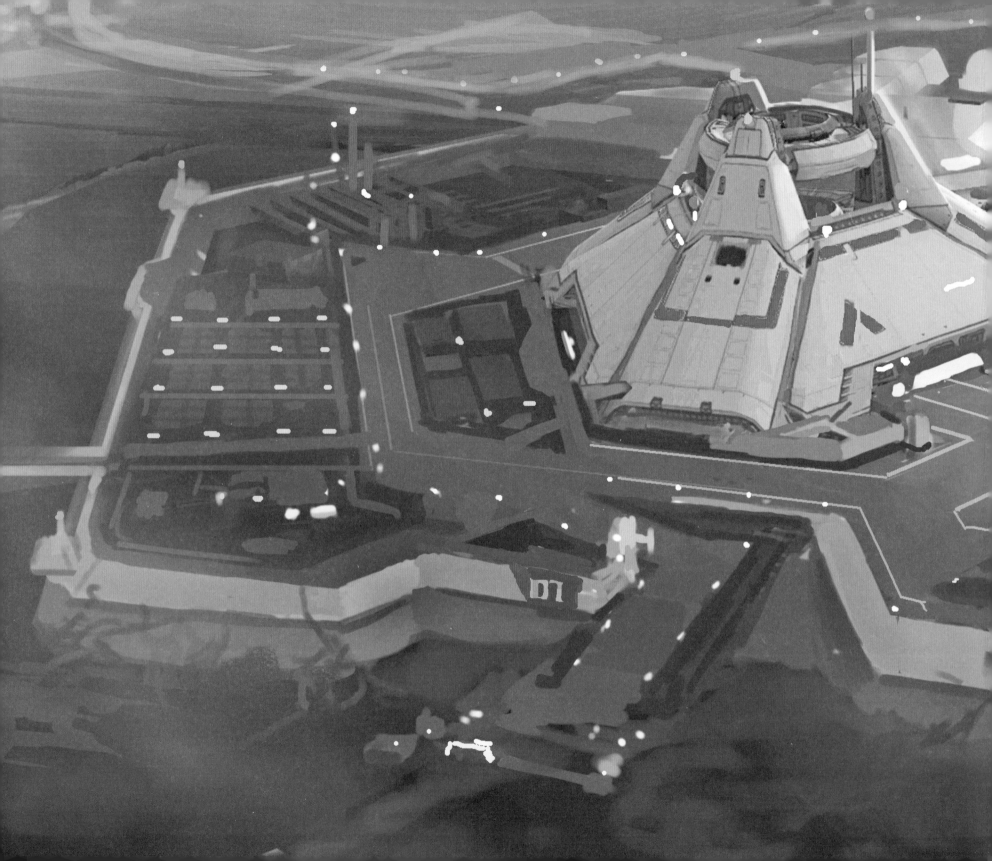